Inflation is Theft

The Foundation for Economic Education, Inc.
Irvington-on-Hudson, New York

Published July 1994
ISBN 0-910614-99-7
Copyright © 1994 by
The Foundation for Economic Education
Irvington-on-Hudson, NY 10533

Table of Contents

Introduction

It is easier to endure losses from error and misjudgment than to sustain damage from injustice. As justice is the crowning glory of all virtues so is injustice the manifest emblem of all evils. It is especially grievous when perpetrated in the name of law or regulation by government officials and agents.

Inflation is a political evil. In the United States it is perpetrated by the officials of the Federal Reserve System in cooperation with agents of the U.S. Treasury. At the very beginning of the country, the Constitution merely gave the Congress the power "to coin money, regulate the value thereof, and of foreign coin... (Article I., Section 8, (5)). In time, the U.S. Congress supported by the Supreme Court interpreted this power to be "legal tender power" in the hands of a monopolistic central bank, the Federal Reserve System.

It is difficult to fathom anything more ominous in monetary matters than a political money monopoly. It permits government authorities to inflate and depreciate the people's money and to force everyone to accept its money at face value. Debtors need not pay their debts in full but can discharge them by giving inferior money in exchange, thereby defrauding the creditors. Legal-tender legislation, which forces everyone to accept the monopoly money in settlement of all debt, public and private, permits government to assess the people without having to seek their consent first, and enables it to live beyond its means and never repay its debt. It is a device of expropriation.

The legal-tender evil came to the United States early in its history. In the name of absolute necessity, the Continental Dollar was made legal tender in 1776; it perished in 1781. During the Civil War, Union greenbacks were given legal tender force. In 1933, all Federal Reserve notes and U.S. Treasury currency were given coercive force. In every case adjudicated by the courts of law the judges ignored the evils and sanctioned the action. The U.S. Supreme court confirmed the legal-tender powers of government in a number of conspicuous decisions. When on June 5, 1933, a Joint Congressional Resolution voided the "gold clause,"

1

2 / *Hans F. Sennholz*

which had set narrow limits to the legal-tender power, the Supreme Court readily sanctioned the revocation, citing the Constitution. In the words of Chief Justice Hughes, "parties cannot remove their transactions from the reach of dominant constitutional power." (Henry Mark Holzer, *Government's Money Monopoly* New York; Books in Focus, 1981, p. 185).

Today, some sixty years later, the "constitutional dollar" is worth less than ten cents of the dollar when the Supreme Court rendered the decision and is losing purchasing power every day. The disastrous nature of this decision becomes apparent when we contemplate the magnitude of the losses which inflation is inflicting on millions of American creditors. Even at the modest rate of three percent depreciation, the annual losses to creditors and gains to debtors now amount to many billions of dollars. Considering such losses on the part of the thrifty and provident, the rising clamor for entitlement and transfer is not surprising. The losses strengthen the demand for Social Security, health care, and many other "cares." They foster federal aid in many forms and otherwise provide a chief argument for an extension of governmental power.

In ages past when gold was legal money and contracts rather than legal-tender force determined monetary relations, an issuer of money substitute was narrowly limited in its power to conduct inflationary policies. When a bank, central bank, or government inflated faster than other issuers it soon lost its reserves of gold, in which all moneys were redeemable, and, to avoid overextension and potential bankruptcy, had to refrain from inflating further. When, in 1971, the United States government had lost most of its reserves of gold, facing some $70 billion in international payment obligations with barely $70 billion of gold in Fort Knox, the U.S. government chose to default rather than halt the inflation. President Richard Nixon renounced the gold obligation as being "unsuited" for international finance, refused to make payment, and thus ushered in a pure paper standard commonly called "fiat."

Having grown accustomed to the U.S. dollar, the world of trade and finance continued to use it without its feature of redeemability. After all, the dollar afforded access to the markets of the most productive country in the world and its record of relative stability was one of the best in recent monetary history despite its devaluations in 1934 and 1971. Above all, the official repudiation of gold created a void which no other fiat currency could possibly fill. It left the U.S. dollar in the most prominent position for becoming the money of the world. It gave rise to the "dollar standard."

The Dollar Standard

International trade and commerce urgently need a reliable medium of exchange. For hundreds of years gold served as the universal money, uniting the world in peaceful cooperation and trade. Today, the U.S. dollar is called upon to assume the very functions of gold. But in contrast to the gold standard, which was rather independent of any one government, the dollar standard depends completely upon the wisdom and discretion of the U.S. monetary authorities; that is, the world standard now rests solely on the forces that shape the monetary policies of the Unites States. It is a political standard in which the purest motives are mixed with the most sordid interests and fiercest passions of the electorate; it is the product of an ideology that places government in charge of the people's money. To expect much of this political handiwork is to invite bitter disappointment.

A fiat standard leads to temptations which no government can be expected to resist. It gives rise to an extraordinary demand for the universal money that tends to support and strengthen its purchasing power. It affords the issuer the rare opportunity to inflate its currency without immediately suffering the dire consequences of currency debasement. In particular, it presents an opportunity to the administration in power to indulge in massive deficit spending, financing it painlessly through currency creation, and for the country to live comfortably beyond its means, enjoying massive imports from abroad while it is exporting the newly created money in payment of such imports. It may suffer balance-of-payment deficits year after year without having to curtail its inflationary habits. In short, it can raise its level of living at the expense of the rest of the world.

For more than two decades the United States has been the great beneficiary of this ominous situation. Year after year the U.S. government has been able to engage in massive deficit spending and currency expansion with minimal inflationary effects as the inflation has been exported to foreign countries. For several years foreign investors even used their dollar earnings to finance large parts of the budgetary deficits of the U.S. government. As the dollar continues to depreciate, the foreigners inevita-

4 / *Hans F. Sennholz*

bly suffer painful losses on their dollar holdings. And yet, they are coming back again and again as long as their own currencies are worse than the U.S. dollar which may be strong in international money markets, even though it is losing purchasing power most of the time. "Strength" in foreign exchange rates merely means relative strength in terms of other currencies that are losing purchasing power even faster. The U.S. dollar may be the strongest currency around although it, too, is continually losing purchasing power; it may rise to spectacular heights versus other currencies although it is sinking to new lows in purchasing power. In recent years it has been losing ground to a few harder currencies such as the Swiss franc, the German mark, and the Japanese yen.

During the 1970s with Presidents Richard Nixon, Gerald Ford, and Jimmy Carter in the White House, the dollar standard nearly floundered. On August 15, 1971 President Nixon launched a three-pronged attack on the dollar by defaulting on all gold-payment obligations to foreign creditors, which instantly weakened the dollar, and by freezing most prices and wages. The freeze severely hampered the production of goods and services and even generated painful shortages in many essential items, aggravating the dollar weakness. At the same time, his administration stoked the fires of inflation through deficit spending and easy-money policies. While an army of price controllers fought hard to keep prices down, another army of Treasury and Federal Reserve officials was busily creating money that raised prices. Although most price controls were lifted gradually in 1974, the deficit spending and credit expansion continued throughout the Ford and Carter years. The sum of currency, demand deposits, travelers checks, and other checkable deposits (M1) rose from $216.6 billion in 1970 to $414.2 billion in 1980. The broader measure of money including certain savings and small time deposits (M2) soared from $682.2 billion to $1,630.3 billion.

Having inflated and depreciated the dollar throughout the decade, the U.S. government soon suffered serious financial embarrassment in international money markets. In October 1979 an international flight from the dollar visibly shook the world dollar standard and cast serious doubt on its future. Gold rose to $850 an ounce and silver to more than $45. The crisis forced President Jimmy Carter to raise $30 billion in harder currencies in order to meet foreign obligations and stem the panic. When the Federal Reserve raised the discount rate to 13 percent with a surcharge of three percent for big banks and the prime rate soared to 25 percent, the crisis finally subsided. Visibly shaken by this experience the Fed subsequently abstained from any further credit expansion which soon led to painful readjustment, the 1981-1982 recession.

During the 1980s, the Reagan era, the U.S. dollar rose and fell, tossed and turned, giving birth to a European movement to cut loose and create an independent European standard. During the recession and for a while thereafter the dollar rose to extraordinary heights which caused more than thirty debtor countries to default on their dollar obligations. When one of the biggest debtors, the government of Mexico, defaulted in August 1982, the U.S. Treasury rushed to its rescue by providing $25 billion in extra funds so that it would pay its creditor banks in New York, Chicago, and Los Angeles. By funding the profligate government of Mexico it rescued the pillars of American banking which had financed the Mexican spending. Later in the decade the U.S. dollar fell again toward the harder currencies, especially the Swiss franc and German mark. It fell precariously because the budgetary deficits of the U.S. government soared to new heights, causing the federal debt to triple during the decade from $907.7 billion in 1980 to $3.233 trillion in 1990. To facilitate the deficits, M1 was made to rise from $414.2 billion to $794.6 billion and M2 from $1,630.3 billion to $3,233.3 billion.

The Reagan decade proved to be extraordinary for several reasons. A number of factors over which the administration had little control greatly reduced the rate of consumer price inflation. The worldwide stagnation threw American agriculture into a deep recession which depressed food prices; similarly, the disintegration of OPEC and the rise of non-OPEC oil production caused energy prices to plummet. Yet, the fiscal deficit and the easy-money policies of the Fed gave rise to an extraordinary international credit expansion. It created a huge credit bubble which allowed the U.S. government to ignore its deficits and continue on its merry way. By the end of the decade the cross-border lending assumed unprecedented proportions which was especially ominous because the debtor countries were wasting the borrowed funds on budget deficits and other binges of consumption.

The international credit bubble grew from the American credit inflation; it was visible in feverish speculation in real estate, corporate mergers, junk bonds, and leveraged takeovers. The fever overwhelmed some

3,000 Savings and Loan Associations and 500 commercial banks which failed during the decade. Squeezed by financial regulation and weakened by rising interest rates, they suffered from disintermediation as depositors moved their funds to unregulated financial institutions. The "deregulation," that is, the relaxation of some rules, came too little too late. It was left to President George Bush to salvage the old structure by placing more than $500 billion of S & L losses on American taxpayers. The Savings and Loan Reform and Rescue Act of August 9, 1989, was passed to re-build the American financial system. It further tightened the regulatory reins, imposed new burdens on taxpayers, reiterated the political commit-ment to economic transfer, and mandated fines and long imprisonment for all violators. Unfortunately, the Act did not alleviate the cause of the evil, it merely changed the labels and shuffled some chairs of the regulators. It changed the names of government agencies and moved the supervision of the thrift industry from the Federal Home Loan Bank Board (FHLBB) directly to the U.S. Treasury. The people's savings henceforth were to be guarded by the arch-enemy of thrift: the U.S. Treasury.

During the 1990s the financial difficulties are likely to multiply. The federal deficits which consumed the lion's share of American savings and much foreign capital during the 1980s are likely to continue. After all, the national elections reveal and confirm the trend. The present adminis-tration in fact is straining to nationalize American healthcare which in time is likely to boost federal expenditures and deficits significantly.

Irritated by their subjection to the dollar standard and their complete exposure to Washington monetary follies, twelve member states of the European Community met in Maastricht, the Netherlands, on December 9-10, 1991, and agreed to create an economic and monetary union, in-cluding a single currency (the ECU) and a European central bank, by the year 1999. The treaty is a European declaration of independence from the United States and the dollar standard. Yet, good intention is hardly sufficient to create a single currency, not to mention dethrone the almighty American dollar. To merge twelve currencies into one and manage it by one supranational authority is to surrender the power to conduct indepen-dent social and economic policies, which are the very raison d'être of modern government. It amounts to an early abolition of the welfare-transfer state.

It is unlikely that the democratic welfare system will survive this cen-tury in their old glory and popularity. Saddled with a heavy burden of politics and unable to compete with the emerging free-market economies, the welfare states are bound to suffer economic stagnation, rising rates of unemployment, and falling wages. The intellectual forces that brought about the disintegration of communism are gnawing also at the foundation of transferism and the political economy. They will bring down the dollar standard which, in the long history of money, will be remembered merely as a short political derangement and departure from what is right and honest. The future belongs to the gold standard, the standard of the ages.

—HANS F. SENNHOLZ

I. IMMORAL POLITICS

Inflationism as Political Policy

by J. H. Peters

The greatest mistake that can be made in economic investigation is to fix attention on mere appearances, and so to fail to perceive the fundamental difference between things whose externals alone are similar, or to discriminate between fundamentally similar things whose externals alone are different.
  —Ludwig von Mises, *The Theory of Money and Credit*

Attempts to penetrate the nation's economic future are engaging the attention of its business and industrial leaders as never before. They are avidly reading and consulting experts in the fields of economics and politics in an endeavor to interpret as accurately as possible all that is happening today in terms of its implications for the future.

But to attempt to read our economic future in projections based on current developments and those of the recent past is a difficult and unproductive undertaking. It is far more to the point to obtain from the reading and contemplation of what has happened over an extended period of economic history an improved knowledge and understanding of what we may do to give that future the shape and direction we want it to take. Samuel Taylor Coleridge said it well sometime during the early years of the nineteenth century: "If man could learn from history, what lessons it might teach us! But passion and party blind our eyes, and the light which experience gives us is a lantern on the stern which shines only on the waves behind us."

We have an unexcelled opportunity to avail ourselves of the lessons of economic history in the many writings of Ludwig von Mises, who predicted the inflation which followed World War I in a work entitled *The Theory of Money and Credit*, the first German-language edition of which

Mr. Peters, former president of the First National Bank of Loveland, Colorado, was for many years the editor of Rand McNally & Company's *Bankers Monthly* magazine. This article appeared in the December 1969 issue of *The Freeman*.

was published in 1912.[1] His writings thus cover a period of nearly sixty years of experimentation with the monetary and fiscal measures invoked by governments in their sundry endeavors to deal with all manner of economic problems. All that follows is based on those of his observations which have a special bearing on the causes of inflation,[2] its consequences, and its sole remedy: stopping the arbitrary expansion of the money supply.

A Pernicious Fallacy Invades Economic Thought

Perhaps the most pernicious idea that has ever invaded the economic thinking of this or any other time is the one that sees inflation as a more or less harmless device by means of which the welfare of all or some segment of the public may be effectively and permanently advanced. And perhaps the most pernicious aspect of that idea lies in the readiness with which it lends itself to the purposes of demagogues who are quite content to promote the adoption of inflationary measures as a means of achieving some momentary political advantage, regardless of what the more remote consequences of their expansionary efforts may prove to be.

Time was when monetary inflation was achieved by employing a single device for a single purpose: the coin of the realm was clipped, and the motive was profit. The government needed financial help and that was the only then known method of tampering with the currency as a means of satisfying that need. Questions of currency policy played no part in the deliberations that prompted it. There was no thought of influencing economic trends or the general price level by manipulating supply and demand factors.

More recently, however, our currency has been debased by a number of devices for a number of reasons, most of them poorly considered and far more harmful than helpful, but nevertheless purportedly rooted in well-intentioned currency policy. The free coinage of silver, for example, was advocated by one group of proponents as a means of increasing the price of silver as a commodity, while the prime concern of another group was to raise the general level of prices by increasing the money supply.

It was through the efforts of the latter that paper inflationism came to be advocated in many states, partly as a forerunner of bimetallism and partly in combination with it. But the closely related issues of monetary policy and inflation were then inadequately comprehended and poorly understood by the public at large, a condition that is all too prevalent to this day.

Although today's currency is nominally based on gold, it actually consists in large part of credit and fiat money, the available quantity of which can be increased or decreased almost at will by our monetary authorities for whatever purposes happen to serve the needs or expediencies of the moment. Every such change is presumed to play a thoroughly considered role in effecting some desired change in the objective exchange-value of the money in circulation.

Indirect Taxation

However valid or otherwise the course pursued to the end in question may be, there remains the problem of the degree to which the prescribed remedy should be applied. To this there can be no precise answer because economists and statisticians have the greatest difficulty in isolating and identifying the determinants of the value of our money, and our federal agencies and lawmakers find it even more difficult, if not impossible, to control them. Inflation, however, lends itself most readily to any effort to engage in painless spending; and because the effects achieved, particularly in the earlier stages of the process, are quite unobjectionable to both the payers and gatherers of taxes, it has at such times gained considerable unwarranted popularity.

Stated differently, the basic cause of inflation lies in government's unwillingness to raise the funds it requires by increasing taxation, or its inability to do so by borrowing from the public. Inflation as a means of financing World War I, for example, had the great advantage of evoking an appearance of both economic prosperity and added wealth. Calculations of every kind were thus falsified, giving rise to distortions in the figures upon which business and industry relied for guidance in the conduct of their affairs. These distortions led, among other things, to the taxing away of portions of the public's capital without its knowledge.

It is thus that political considerations all too often interfere with the proper functioning of one phase or another of the economic process. Left to its own devices, the economy has a way of effecting its own cures of maladjustments as they arise. If its pricing mechanism is permitted to reflect without outside interference the extent and urgency of the needs and wants of the public, supply and demand will inevitably arrive at a condition of balance.

It is generally supposed that inflation favors the debtor at the expense of the creditor, but this is true only if and to the extent that the reduction in the value of money is unforeseen. Inflationary policy can alter the relations between creditor and debtor in favor of the latter only if it takes effect suddenly and unexpectedly.

If, on the other hand, inflation is foreseen, those who lend money will feel obliged to include in the rate of interest they ask both a rate that will compensate them for the loss to be expected on account of the depreciation actually anticipated, and as much more as might result from a *less* probable further depreciation. And any who hesitate to pay this additional compensation will find that the diminished supply of funds available in the loan market will compel them to do so. Savings deposits, incidentally, decreased during the inflation that followed World War I because savings banks were not inclined to adjust interest rates to the altered conditions created by variations in the purchasing power of money.

Supposed Benefits of Inflation Are Illusions

There are inflationists who, though they are admittedly quite aware of the evils of inflation, nevertheless hold that there are higher and more important aims of economic policy than a sound monetary system. A failure on the part of the public to comprehend all of the implications of the position thus taken makes inflation a readily available political expedient. When governments are relieved of the necessity for making ends meet, socialistic trends and other unpopular consequences of a given policy are all too readily concealed in order to win and hold the required degree of public acceptance; and having arrived at that point, arrival at a condition of absolutism is only a question of time.

There isn't a shred of validity in the proposition that continued inflation is to be preferred to any steps that might be taken with a view to counteracting it; in the notion, for example, that increased unemployment in any degree would be too large a price to pay for a stabilized price structure. Quite ignored in this view of the matter is the consideration that stabilized or increased employment obtained temporarily at the price of inflation is a very poor bargain indeed, and that the effect of that continuing process can only be to give rise to an accumulation of economic maladjustments that must eventually fall of its own weight.

It will be recalled that the nation's economic situation in 1934 was quite the reverse of today's. Employment was at a very low level, but governments around the world were dealing with it altogether unrealistically. Instead of adjusting wages to the generally prevailing low level of prices, they sought to ward off a fall in money wages and otherwise interfered with the processes that would have restored the economy to a condition of equilibrium in the natural course of events.

They ignored the unwelcome truth that by stabilizing wages at an arbitrarily high level they were actually increasing unemployment and perpetuating the disproportion then existing between prices and costs and between outputs and sales, the predominant symptoms of the crisis with which they were contending. Just as an inflated wage structure stood in the way of needed adjustments when the economy was at a low ebb, it will inevitably be found to have much the same effect when attempts finally are made to curb the malinvestments generated by boom conditions.

Subjective Value of Money

Contributing to the difficulties just cited are, first of all, the multitudinous factors that influence the objective exchange-value of money, popularly called its purchasing power. But its *subjective* exchange value is also important. Just as in the case of economic goods, the economic valuation of money is based on subjective estimates of individuals as prompted by their psychological reactions to whatever circumstances and conditions may happen to obtain in their respective situations. Subjective value, therefore, cannot be determined with even a modicum of accuracy, and any decision based on an assumed ability to do so is sure to be highly conjectural, to say the very least.[3]

It is clear, therefore, that inflation functions quite inadequately as a purely political instrument. Its effects cannot be predicted with any degree of precision, and if continued indefinitely it must lead to a collapse. Its popularity is due in the main to the public's inability to fully understand its consequences.

Barriers to Reversal

Standing in sharp contrast to the great ease with which a policy of inflation may be used by those in authority for their own purposes is the great difficulty of reversing that process—of invoking and implementing a policy of restrictionism or restraint which has the effect of increasing the value of money. This may be done (1) by reducing the supply of money in a period of constant demand, or (2) by holding it at a uniform level or one that is insufficiently high to meet anticipations based on recent price trends. The latter less severe method consists in simply waiting for an increase in the demand for a limited supply of money to manifest as a condition of restraint.

Adding to the difficulty of pursuing a policy of restraint are these considerations.

1. Far from bringing to the national Treasury the added dollar resources to which inflation too readily gives rise, restraint diminishes them.

2. It tends to induce a scarcity of some economic goods by facilitating exports and restricting imports.

3. Taxation becomes more burdensome.

4. Unpopular creditors, as a class, are thought to gain at the expense of the far more numerous debtors. (Today in the United States, the large corporations tend to be the debtors, while the creditors by and large are numerous small savers with insurance, savings accounts, and the like.)

Redeemability

But every inflationary policy must sooner or later be abandoned, and there will then remain the problem of replacing it with another. It was the clear intent of the law in the first place to preserve the metal parity of our currency, and that can be the only legally and morally acceptable objective of the new policy. Suspension of convertibility left that premise altogether unchanged.

The inflation made possible by the suspension of convertibility, however, has already worked grave inequities in contractual relations of every kind, and to abandon metal parity in the formulation of a new policy could only serve to make bad matters worse. Although the consequences of inflation cannot be eliminated by a mere reversal of policy, and existing inequities would in large part remain, metal parity would at least hold more promise of future stability than any available alternative.

Even so, the value of our currency will be too largely subject to political pressure, and it is to be hoped that the electorate will see to it that a preponderance of such pressure is exerted in behalf of a stable currency. For it is, after all, no part of the proper function of government to influence the value of the medium of exchange. That is the function of the market, in the use and operation of which government is only one of many participants. It is to the market itself that all must look for the means of establishing the relative exchange values of economic goods, and government has, or should have, little actual voice in the matter.

The result of any attempted intervention by government will be determined in large part by the subjective values placed on goods by the masses of participating individuals through the pricing process. While our monetary authorities have some knowledge of the factors that determine the value of money, they have no way of determining the extent to which subjective estimates of value (prices) are affected by variations in the quantity of money. Governmental intervention is therefore confronted with the impossible problem of calculating the intensity with which variations in the ratio of the supply of money to the demand for it affect the market.

The Evils of Price Control

The adoption of price and wage ceilings is frequently suggested as a means of controlling inflation, but history's case against that course is devastatingly complete. Such ceilings would automatically stimulate demand for and curtail production of the very goods that happened to be in scarce supply. The mechanism of the market would no longer be effective in allocating available supplies, so it would be necessary to bring other forces to bear on the problem. These have historically led through various intermediate stages, beginning with the rationing of the most important necessities, to the eventual abolition of private property. There is no workable substitute for the age-old laws of supply and demand.

And so it is with the balance of international payments. If natural forces are permitted to function without interference, the tighter money conditions which will normally prevail in the debtor country will induce a reduction in its prices, thus discouraging imports and encouraging exports, and thereby tending to bring about a restoration of equilibrium. The government in question can best serve its own needs by refraining from intervention of any kind.

The role of the speculator is a further case in point. In times long past the activity of speculators was held to be responsible for the depreciation of money; but, here again, history makes it clear that prices are determined in the market, and that any attempt to alter them over a given period by speculation is sure to fail; that the immediate effect of speculation is to reduce price fluctuations rather than to increase them. In the case of a steadily weakening currency, however, the effect of speculation will be to cause the expected depreciation to depart from its otherwise uniform pattern, and to proceed by fits and starts, with intermittent pauses. But the framework will be set by the extent to which market factors are responsible for the decline; and if inflation happens to be the cause of the difficulty, it is to the cure of that malady that all corrective efforts must be directed.

We are faced with a choice between the forces that make for monetary stability and those that will inevitably take us in the opposite direction. We can't have it both ways.

---

1. The first English edition of a version written in 1924 appeared in the 1930s, and the book, to which was added a then-current essay on "Monetary Reconstruction," was last published in 1953.

2. Mises indicates a strong preference for the use of "inflationism" as the only term that conveys the precise meaning intended. He defines "inflationism" as "that monetary policy that seeks to increase the quantity of money," whereas "inflation" is said to mean an increase in the quantity of money (in the broader sense of the term, so as to include fiduciary media as well), that is not offset by a corresponding increase in the need for money (again in the broader sense of the term) so that a fall in the objective exchange-value of money must occur." He makes the further point that inflationism must occur on a very substantial scale before it will manifest as inflation in the ordinarily accepted sense of the term. "Inflationism," in other words, may be said to be the policy that tends to induce "inflation." In the present situation, the policy and its effect appear to be generally regarded as one and the same.

3. An article entitled "Psychology and the Consumer," which appeared in the August 1969, issue of *Business in Brief,* published by The Chase Manhattan Bank of New York, strongly supports this view. The author variously described the consumer as a "hero," a "villain," and a "victim," the respective roles played by him in (1) the 1965-66 period of caution, (2) the period of excessive optimism which got under way at the beginning of 1967, and (3) in the current year of disregard of the restraints on consumer spending which it was sought to impose by the boost in Social Security taxes and the tax surcharge. Notwithstanding the latter, "for 1968 as a whole, consumer outlays were 9.0 percent above 1967—significantly contributing to inflationary pressure."

The Moral Issue of Honest Money

by Gary North

Because of the nature of the economics profession—"guild" might be a better word—it is necessary to put quotation marks around the words, "honest money." Economists will go to almost any lengths to avoid the use of moral terms when they discuss economic issues. This has been true since the seventeenth century, when early mercantilistic pamphlet writers tried to avoid religious controversy by creating the illusion of moral and religious neutrality in their writings. This, they falsely imagined, would produce universal agreement, or at least more readily debatable disagreements, since "scientific" arguments are open to rational investigation. The history of both modern science and modern economics since the seventeenth century has demonstrated how thoroughly unreconcilable the scientists are, morality or no morality.

Nevertheless, traditions die hard. Economists are not supposed to inject questions of morality into their analyses. Economics is still supposedly a "positive" science, one concerned strictly with questions of "if . . . then." *If* the government does A, then B is likely to result. *If* the government wants to achieve D, *then* it should adopt policy E. The economist is completely neutral, of course. He is just an observer who deals with means of achieving ends. The economist can therefore deal with "complete neutrality," with this sort of problem: "If the Nazis wish to exterminate 50,000 people, which are the most cost-effective means?" No morality, you understand, just simple economic analysis.

The problem with the theory of neutral economics is that people are not neutral, effects of government policies are not neutral, social systems are not neutral, legal systems are not neutral, and when pressed, even economists are not neutral. Because societies are not neutral, the costs of violating a society's first principles have to be taken into account. But no economist can do any more than guess about such costs. There is no

© Gary North, 1982. Dr. Gary North, is President of the Institute for Christian Economics, Tyler, Texas. This article is reprinted with permission of the author from the February 1982 issue of *The Freeman*.

known way to assess the true costs to society of having its political leaders defy fundamental moral principles and adopt any given policy. And if
the economists guess wrong—not an unlikely prospect, given the hypothetical moral vacuum in which economists officially operate—then the
whole society will pay. (This assumes, of course, that policy-makers listen to economists.)

The inability of economists to make accurate cost-benefit analyses of
any and all policy matters is a kind of skeleton in the profession's closet.
The problem was debated back in the late 1930s, and a few economists
still admit that it is a real theoretical problem, but very few think about it.
The fact of the matter is simple: *there is no measuring device for balancing total individual utility vs. total disutility for society as a whole.*
You cannot, as a scientist, make interpersonal comparisons of subjective
utility. The better economists know this, but they prefer not to think about
it. They want to give advice, but as scientists they cannot say what policy
is better for society as a whole.[1]

This is why politicians and policy-makers have to rely on *intuition,*
just as the economists do. There is no scientific standard to tell them
whether or not a particular policy should be imposed. Without a concept
of morality—that some policy is morally superior to another—the economists' "if . . . then" game will not answer the questions that need to be
answered. *Without moral guidelines, there is little hope of guessing correctly concerning the true costs and benefits to society as a whole of any
policy.* The economist, as a scientist, is in no better position to make such
estimations than anyone else. If anything, he is in a worse position, since
his academic training has conditioned him to avoid mixing moral issues
and economic analysis. He is not used to dealing with such questions.

What Is Honest Money?

Honest money is a social institution that arises from honest dealings
among acting individuals. Money is probably best defined as *the most
marketable commodity.* I accept a dollar in exchange for goods or services that I supply only because I have reason to suspect that someone
else will do the same for me later on. If I begin to suspect that others will
refuse to take my dollar in exchange for their goods and services in the
future, I will be less willing to take that dollar today. I may ask the buyer

to pay me a dollar and a quarter, just to compensate me for my risk in holding that dollar over time.

A currency unit functions as money—a medium of *voluntary* exchange—only because people expect it to do so in the *future*. One reason why they expect a particular currency unit to be acceptable in the future is that it has been acceptable in the past. A monetary unit has to have *historic* value in most instances, if it is to function as money. Occasionally, meaning very rarely, a government can impose a new currency unit on its citizens, and sometimes this works. One good example is the introduction of the new German mark in November of 1923, which was exchanged for the old mark at a trillion to one. But normally the costs are so high in having people rethink and relearn a new currency unit that governments avoid such an imposition.

Historic Stability

The question policy-makers must ask themselves is this: To avoid the necessity of imposing a totally new currency unit on a population, what can be done to convince people that the future usefulness of the currency in voluntary exchange will remain high? What can be done to improve the historic value of money in the future? In other words, when people in a year or a decade look back at the performance of their nation's currency unit, will they say to themselves: "This dollar that I'm holding today buys pretty much what it bought back then. I think it's safe for me to continue to accept dollars in exchange for my goods and services, since people trust its buying power. I have no reason to believe that its purchasing power will fall in the future, so I can take the risk of accepting payment in dollars today." If people do not say this to themselves, then the dollar's purchasing power is undermined. People will demand more dollars in payment, meaning prices will go up, if they *suspect that* prices will go up. This, in turn, convinces more people that the historic value of their money has been unreliable, which then leads to higher prices.

The economist will tell you that prices cannot continue to go up unless the government, working with the central bank, accommodates price inflation by expanding the currency base. The economist is correct in the long run, whatever the long run is these days, or will be in a few years. *But governments have a pernicious tendency to accommodate price inflation.* Dr. Arthur Burns was forthright about this back in 1976:

These days the Federal Reserve is now and then described as pursuing a restrictive monetary policy. The Federal Reserve is described as being engaged in a struggle against inflation. The Federal Reserve is even charged with being more concerned about inflation than about unemployment, which is entirely false. It is by generating inflation, or permitting inflation, that we get unemployment on a massive scale eventually. But let us in the Federal Reserve ask this question: Are we accommodating inflation at the present time or not? The answer—the only honest, professional answer—is that, to a large degree, we are accommodating the inflation; in other words, are making it possible for inflation to continue.[2]

So we get a kind of self-fulfilling prophecy. The government expands the money supply in order to finance its deficits, or create a temporary economic boom, or whatever, and the prices for goods and services rise. Everyone in the "great American auction" has more dollars to use in the bidding process, so prices rise. Then the public gets suspicious about the future value of money, because they have seen the loss of purchasing power in the past. They demand higher prices. Then the Federal Reserve System is encouraged by politicians to accommodate the price inflation, in order to keep the boom going (to keep the "auction" lively). The dollar loses its *present* value, because it has lost its *historic* value, which encourages people to discount sharply its *future* value.

The secret of retaining the public's confidence in any currency unit is simple enough: *convince users of the money that the issuers are responsible, reliable, and trustworthy.* Government and its licensed agents have a monopoly of money creation. Private competitors are called counterfeiters. Sadly, in our day, it is very difficult to understand just what it is that counterfeiters do, economically speaking, that governments are not already doing. Fiat money is fiat money. (Perhaps the real legal issue ought to be the illegal use of the government's copyrighted material. *Copyright infringement* makes a much more logical case for Federal prosecution than counterfeiting.)

Who Guards the Guardians?

There is an ancient question that every society must answer: "Who guards the guardians?" Or in more contemporary usage, "Who referees the referees?" The public needs *an impersonal guardian to* restrain the actions of those who hold a legal monopoly of money creation: the government, the central bank, and the commercial banks. The public can guard the guardians if citizens have the right to go down to the local bank and receive payment in gold, silver, or some other money metal. The issuers of money need only stamp on the paper money (or check, or deposit book entry) that the holder of the currency unit has a legal right to redeem his *warehouse receipt* for a stated weight and fineness of a specific metal.[3] Whenever the issuing agencies begin to issue more receipts than they have reserves of metal, the public has the option of "calling the bluff" of the issuers, and demanding payment, as promised by law. It is this restraint—implicit economically, but explicit legally—which serves as the impersonal guardian of the public trust.

The government can always change the law. Governments do this all the time. Whenever there is a major war, for example, governments suspend specie payments. They also suspend civil liberties, and for the same reason: to increase the power of the state at the expense of the citizens. Governments in peacetime are frequently unwilling to reestablish pre-war taxes, pre-war civil liberties, and pre-war convertibility of currencies, long after the war is over. Civil libertarians have not generally understood *the case for a gold standard as a case for civil liberties,* despite the obvious historical correlation between wartime suspension of civil liberties and wartime suspension of specie payments.

When the authorities declare the convertibility of paper into specie metals "null and void," it sends the public a message. "Attention! This is your government speaking. We are no longer willing to subject ourselves to your continual interference in our governmental affairs. We no longer can tolerate illegitimate restrictions on our efforts to guard the public welfare, especially from the public. Therefore, we are suspending the following civil right: the public's legal right to call our bluff when we guarantee free convertibility of our currency. This should not be interpreted as an immoral act on the part of the government. Contracts are not moral issues. They are strictly pragmatic. However, we assure you, from the bottom of our collective heart, that we shall never expand the money supply, or allow the historic value of the currency to depreciate. It will be just as if we had a gold standard restraint on our printing presses. However, such restraints are unnecessary, and besides, they are altogether too restraining."

Redeemability Required

Critics of the gold standard tell us that the value of any currency is dependent on public confidence, not gold. But what the critics refuse to admit is that the existence of *the civil liberty of redeemable money* is an important psychological support of the public's confidence in money. Even when the public does not understand the gold standard's theoretical justification—an impersonal guard of the monopolistic guardians—citizens can exercise their judgment on a daily basis by either demanding payment in gold (or silver, or whatever) or not demanding payment. Like the free market itself, it works whether or not the bulk of the participants understand the theory. What they do understand is self-interest: if there is a profit to be made from buying gold at the official rate, and selling it into the free market (including foreign markets) at a higher price, then some people will enter the markets as middlemen, "buying low and selling high," until the government realizes that its bluff has been called, and it therefore is forced to reduce the expansion of the money supply.

What is the morality of a gold standard? Simple: it is *the morality of a legal contract.* A government's word is its bond. A government promises to restrain itself in the creation of money, in order to assure citizens that the monopoly of money-creation will not be abused by those holding the monopoly grant of power. The *gold standard* is very much like a *constitution:* an impersonal, reliable institution which has as its premier function the counterbalancing of potentially damaging monopolistic power.

"Flexible" Money

Flexible money is a euphemism for the government's ability to increase (but, historically speaking, rarely to decrease) the money supply. The degree of flexibility is determined by the political process, not by the direct response of those affected, namely, individual citizens who would otherwise have the right to demand payment in gold. Flexible money means monetary inflation. Very flexible money means a whole lot of monetary inflation. Monetary inflation means, within 24 months, price inflation.

Civil libertarians instantly recognize the danger of "flexible administrative law," or "flexible censorship," or "flexible enforcement of speed traps." Yet they have great difficulty in recognizing precisely the same kind of evil in "flexible monetary policy." The threat comes from the same institution, the civil government. It comes for the same reasons: the desire of the government to increase its arbitrary exercise of monopolistic power over the citizenry, and to limit public resistance.

The inflationary implications of "flexible monetary policy" can be seen in a revealing exchange between Arthur Burns and Henry Reuss:

> *Dr. Burns*: Let me say this, if I may: the genius of monetary policy—its great virtue—is that it is flexible. With respect to the growth ranges that we project for the coming year, as I have tried to advise this committee from time to time—and as I keep reminding others, including members of my own Federal Reserve family—our goal at the Federal Reserve is not to make a particular projection come true; our goal is to adjust what we do with a view to achieving a good performance of the economy. If at some future time I should come to this committee and report a wide discrepancy between our projection and what actually happened in the sphere of money and credit, I would not be embarrassed in the slightest. On the contrary, I would feel that the Federal Reserve had done well and I would even anticipate a possible word of praise from this generous committee.

> *Chairman Reuss*: You would get it, and the word of praise would be even louder and more deeply felt if you came up and said that due to the change in circumstances you were proving once again that you were not locked on automatic pilot and were willing to become more expansive if the circumstances warranted. Either way you would get praise beyond belief.[4]

Praise beyond belief! Who wants anything less? Just take the monetary system off "automatic pilot," and turn it over to those whose *short-run political goals* favor a return of the inflation-generated economic boom, once the boom has worn off because the printing presses are not *accelerating* the output of fiat money—fiat money being defined as former warehouse receipts for metal, in which even the pretense of a warehouse has been abandoned. *Gold is a tough-minded automatic pilot.*

Politically, there is a great deal of flexibility in monetary affairs. Few people even pretend to understand monetary affairs, and most of those who do really do not understand the logic of the gold standard. The logic is very simple, very clear, and universally despised: *It is cheaper to print money than it is to dig gold.*

Problems with Fiat Money

Fiat money is indeed more flexible than gold, especially in an upward direction. Fiat money allows the government to spend newly manufactured money into circulation. It allows those who gain early access to the newly created fiat money to go out and buy up scarce economic resources at *yesterday's prices*—prices based on supply and demand conditions that were being bid in terms of yesterday's money supply. But this leads to some important problems.

1. Yesterday's prices will climb upward to adjust for today's money supply.
2. People will begin to have doubts about the stability of tomorrow's prices.
3. Producers and sellers of resources may begin to discount the future purchasing power of today's dollar (that is, hike today's prices in anticipation).
4. The government or central bank will be severely tempted to "accommodate" rising prices by expanding the money supply.
5. And the beat goes on.

Paying for the Guards

It is quite true, as Milton Friedman has stated so graphically, that the gold standard is expensive.[5] We dig gold out of the ground in one location, only to bury it in the ground in another location. We cannot do this for free. Wouldn't it be more efficient, meaning less wasteful of scarce economic resources, Dr. Friedman asks, just to forget about digging up gold? Why not keep the government or the central bank from expanding the money supply? Then the same ends could be accomplished so much less wastefully. Save resources: trust politicians.

This is a very strange argument, coming as it does from a man who understands the efficiency of market processes, as compared to political and bureaucratic processes. The gold standard is the way that individual citizens, acting to increase their own personal advantage, can profit from any monetary inflation on the part of the monetary authorities. They can "buy low and sell high" simply by exchanging paper money for gold at the undervalued, official exchange rate, and hoarding gold in expectation of a higher price, or selling it into the free market at a higher price. Why is the price higher? Because individuals expect the government to go back on its promise, raise the official price of gold (that is, devalue the currency unit), or close the gold window altogether. Citizens can become future-predicting, risk-bearing, uncertainty-bearing speculators in a very restricted market, namely, *the market for government promises.* It allows those who are skeptical about the trustworthiness of government promises to take a profit-seeking position in the market. It allows those who trust the government to deposit money at 6 percent or 10 percent or whatever. Each side can speculate concerning the trustworthiness of government promises concerning redeemability of the currency, or more to the point, government promises concerning the future stability of the currency unit's purchasing power.

Let the Market Function

Defenders of the commodity futures markets—and this includes Dr. Friedman—argue that the existence of a market for future delivery and future payment of commodities smooths out market prices, since it opens the market to those who are willing to bear the uncertainties of predicting the future. Those who are successful predictors increase their profits, and therefore increase their strength in establishing market prices according to the true future conditions of supply and demand. Those who are less successful soon are forced out of the futures markets, thereby passing along capital to those who are more successful predictors. The public is served well by such markets, for obvious reasons. Prices adjust to future consumer demand more rapidly, since accurate future-predictors are being rewarded in these markets.

Then why not a market for future government promises? Why not a market which can test the government's willingness to deliver a stated quantity and fineness of gold or silver (but preferably gold, given international exchange)? The monopolists who control the money supply then are faced with a market which offers rewards to those who are willing and able to "call the monopolists' bluff" and demand gold for the government's warehouse receipts.

Why not just rely on the standard commodity contracts for gold in the commodity futures markets? Won't skeptics be able to take their profits this way? Why bring in the "spurious" issue of a convertible currency? The answer is simple enough: once society has given a monopoly to the government to create money, then the full redeemability of the currency unit is a direct, immediately felt restriction on government power. Of course the free market in commodities allows speculators to take advantage of monetary inflation, if their timing is correct. But this does not mean that the public at large will exercise effective action to force a political change in present monetary policy. There is no immediate self-interest involved in expending resources in what could prove to be a fruitless, expensive campaign to stop the inflation.

Fixing the Responsibility

In the commodities market, one investor wins, and one investor loses (unless the price stays the same, in which case only the broker wins). By establishing the gold standard—full redeemability of gold on public demand—the government forces the Treasury to risk becoming an immediate, measurable loser. It forces the Treasury's officials to come back to the politicians and announce, "Folks, we have lost the bet. The public has called our bluff. They have drained us of our gold. We can't go on much longer. We have to stop the inflation. We have to convince the public to start trusting the currency, meaning that they should start trusting our competence in securing them a currency with a future. We have to balance the budget. Stop inflating!"

An open commodities market in gold is desirable, of course. But it is no substitute for a gold standard, if the state has a monopoly of money creation (along with its licensed subcontractors, the banks). Unless there is full redeemability, the Treasury is not forced by law to "go long" on its promises whenever anyone else wants to "go short."

Without full redeemability, the Treasury, meaning the government, can keep on shorting its own promises, despite the response of organized commodities markets, until an expensive and successful political campaign can be launched to stabilize the money supply. As free market analysis tells us, these campaigns are expensive to launch because of such factors as information costs, costs of organizing pressure groups, and the lack of an immediate, short-run pay-off to "investors" who contribute money to such a program. Full redeemability allows market forces to work. Self-interested forecasters can speculate in the government promises market. The public never has to be told to vote, or send letters of protest, or do anything. The self-interested speculators—a small but well-capitalized elite—will do the "policing" job for the citizens free of charge.[6] (Well, almost: there are transaction costs.)

So when we are told that it is inefficient to dig gold out of the ground, only to deposit it in a vault, we are not being told the whole story. By tying the currency unit to that gold which is wonderfully expensive to mine, as any *monetary brake* should be and must be, the body politic enlists a cadre of professional, self-interested speculators to serve as an *unpaid police force*. This police force polices the trustworthiness of government monetary promises. The public can relax, knowing that a hard core of greedy capitalists is at work for the public interest, monitoring federal budgets, Federal Reserve policies, and similarly arcane topics. By forcing the Treasury to "go long" in its own *promises market,* the guardians are guarded by the best guards of all: future-predicting, self-interested speculators whose job it is *to embarrass those who do not honor contracts*—monetary contracts.

Conclusions

I suppose I could invest more time in presenting graphs, or faking some impressive-looking equations, or citing innumerable forgotten defenders of the gold standard. But I think I have reached the point of diminishing returns. The logic of the gold standard is really fairly simple: *Treasury monopolists, like all other monopolists, cannot be trusted to honor their promises.* Better put, they cannot be trusted *at zero cost.* The gold standard is one relatively inexpensive way to impose high costs on government monetary officials who do not honor their implicit contracts with the body politic to monitor and deliver a reliable currency unit that will have future value—a trustworthy money system.

There are *moral* issues involved: honoring contracts, preserving social stability, providing a trustworthy government. There are *civil liberties* issues involved: protecting citizens from unwarranted taxation through monetary inflation, protecting citizens from arbitrary (read: "flexible") monetary policies, and restricting the expansion of government power. There are *economic* issues involved: designing an institutional mechanism that will bring self-interest to bear on political-economic policies, to stabilize purchasing power, to increase the spread of information in the community, and to increase the political risks for money monopolists. No doubt, I could go on, but these arguments seem sufficient.

The real question is more fundamental: Do we trust governments *or* the high costs of mining precious metals? William McChesney Martin, Dr. Burns' predecessor as Chairman of the Federal Reserve Board, gave us the options back in 1968, in the midst of an international monetary crisis: "It's governments that you have to rely on. Basically, you can't rely on a metal for solvency."[7]

Those of us who cannot bring ourselves to trust the government with any monopoly over the control of money prefer to trust a metal. It may not be the best thing to trust, but it is certainly more reliable than governments.

Keeping Government Honest

The case for a gold standard is the case against arbitrary civil government. While politicians may well resent "automatic pilots" in the sphere of monetary policy, if we had a more automatic pilot, we would have less intensive "boom-bust" cycles. When the "automatic pilot" is subject to tinkering by politicians or Federal Reserve officials, then it is not automatic any longer.

The appeal of specie metals is not the lure of magical talismans, as some critics of gold seem to imply. Gold is not a barbarous relic. Gold is a metal which, over millennia, has become acceptable as a means of payment in a highly complex institutional arrangement: the monetary system. Gold is part of civilization's most important economic institution, the division-of-labor-based monetary system. Without this division of labor, which monetary calculation has made possible, most of the world's population would be dead within a year, and probably within a few weeks. The alternative to the free market social order is government tyranny, some military-based centralized allocation system. Any attempt by the state to alter men's voluntary decisions in the area of exchange, including their choice of exchange units, represents the true relic of barbarism, namely, the use of force to determine the outcome of men's decisions.

The gold standard offers men an alternative to the fiat money systems that have transferred massive monopolistic power to the civil government. The gold standard is not to be understood as a restraint on men's freedom, but just the opposite: a means of restraining that great enemy of freedom, the arbitrary state. A gold standard restores an element of *impersonal predictability* to voluntary exchange—impersonal in the limited sense of not being subject to the whims of any individual or group. This predictability helps to reduce the uncertainties of life, and therefore helps to reduce the costs of human action. It is not a zero-cost institution, but it has proven itself as an important means of reducing arbitrary government. It is an "automatic pilot" which the high-flying, loud-crashing political daredevils resent. That, it seems to me, is a vote in its favor.

---

1. For those who are curious shout this great debate over the impossibility of making interpersonal comparisons of subjective utility, see the exchange that took place between Sir Roy Harrod and Lionel Robbins: Roy K. Harrod, "Scope and Methods of Economics," *The Economic Journal* (September, 1938) and Lionel Robbins, "Interpersonal Comparisons of Utility: A Comment," *The Economic Journal* (December, 1938). For some "New Left" conclusions concerning the results of this debate, see Mark A. Lutz and Kenneth Lux, *The Challenge of Humanistic Economics* (Menlo Park, Calif.: Benjamin Cummings, 1979), pp. 83-89. For my own observations on its implications, see Gary North, *The Dominion Covenant: Genesis* (Tyler, Texas: Institute for Christian Economics, 1982), ch. 4.

2. *Federal Rescue Consultations on the Conduct of Monetary Policy,* Hearings Before the Committee on Banking, Currency and Housing, House of Representatives, 94th Congress, 2nd Session (July 27 and 28, 1976), pp. 26-27. Printed by the U.S. Government Printing Office, Washington, D.C.

3. On money as a warehouse receipt, see Murray N. Rothbard, *Man, Economy and State* (New York: New York University Press, [1962] 1975), pp. 700-703.

4. *Federal Reserve Consultations,* p. 13.

5. Writes Professor Friedman: "My conclusion is that an automatic commodity standard is neither a feasible nor a desirable solution to the problem of establishing monetary arrangements for a free society. It is not desirable because it would involve a large cost in the form of resources used to produce the monetary commodity." *Capitalism and Freedom* (Chicago: University of Chicago Press, 1962), p. 42.

6. "By creating monitors with a vested interest in the maximization of a given set of values, property rights reduce the social cost of monitoring efficiency." Thomas Sowell, *Knowledge and Decisions* (New York: Basic Books, 1980), p. 125.

7. William McChesney Martin, quoted in the *Los Angeles Times* (March 19, 1968), Pt. 1, p. 12.

Built-In Pressures to Inflation

by Clarence B. Carson

All the obligations of the U. S. government, both actual and potential, stand today as pressures toward inflation. They are like a vast sea lapping at, thrusting against, and threatening to crash through the defenses built against it by a succession of casually thrown up dikes. Indeed, the momentum lies with inflation, and the pressures mount with each new obligation undertaken and every old obligation that comes to maturity.

Inflation is used in two somewhat distinct ways today. It is used by some economic thinkers to refer to the increase of the money supply. Popularly, it is used to refer to general rises in prices. If it be understood that the increase of the money supply is the cause of the general price rise, much of the objection to the second usage is removed. Not all of it, however. There would still be an unmeasurable phenomenon with no name and no way to identify it if inflation could apply only to general rises in prices. The reason is this: It is possible to have increases in the money supply accompanied by no general price increases. Indeed, it is conceivable that over some period of time increases in the money supply might be accompanied by a slight decline in prices. There may be a variety of reasons for such effects. The additional money might have gone into savings. There may have been productivity increases which offset the increases in the money supply. (In which case prices would have fallen, or fallen more than they did, had the money supply not been increased.) In any case, if inflation refers only to increases in prices, it will only be noted when prices actually increase. More importantly, if inflation refers only to price increases, it may be, and frequently is, separated from its basic cause— increases of the money supply by government. For these reasons, inflation is used here to refer to increases in the money supply.

Dr. Carson has written and taught extensively, specializing in American intellectual history. This article is reprinted from the September 1976 issue of *The Freeman*.

A Form of Taxation

The effect of inflation, whether it results in a measurable increase in prices or not, is that it levies a tax on all who have money or have it owed to them. It reduces the value of the currency, and the amount of that reduction is used by government to pay its bills. In the United States today, the government inflates by monetizing debt, its own debt directly and other debt more indirectly. The only limits to the money supply are arbitrary reserve requirements on banks and changing debt limits set by Congress. These are the thin and flexible dikes holding back the onrushing sea of inflation.

What are these pressures to inflation? The most obvious one, of course, is the national debt. It has now reached or passed $600 billion [1976]. The debt presses us toward inflation in two ways. One is by way of paying the interest on it. The annual interest on the debt is now in the $30-40 billion rate, and has lately been rising more rapidly in proportion than the national debt. The interest must be paid from taxes or by inflation. An even stronger pressure to inflation is the continual refinancing of portions of the debt. The debt is not being retired but it is being continually paid off and renewed as bonds and other securities mature or are cashed by their holders. This is inflationary to the extent that the refinancing is by way of monetizing the debt. In a similar fashion, any growth in the debt is likely to be inflationary.

But the national debt is only the best known and most obvious obligation of the United States government. It is actually only the exposed tip of the iceberg of obligations. Among these, the obligations under Social Security may be the next best well known. From time to time, calculations are made as to the extent of Social Security obligations. None of these need detain us, however, for they are only projections based on current payments, commitments, and longevity expectations. Since cost-of-living adjustments are now made regularly, Congress periodically adds new benefits, and the number covered is expanded, there is no way to calculate the amount of the obligation. Suffice it to say, the obligation is immense and the amount of it rapidly rising.

Social Security Deficits

Social Security is already beginning to exercise inflationary pressure. For most of its history it did not do so. Income into the program exceeded the payments out of it. A "fund" was being built up. More specifically, Social Security payments were helping to finance the national debt. Now, however, that has changed. Social Security is paying out more than it is taking in. The difference is being made up by the sale of government securities. For the time being, the result will not necessarily be any net increase in the debt, but it will bring on inflation to the extent that the debt is refinanced by monetizing it. This inflationary pressure will mount to the extent that the gap between intake and outgo widens. When and if the "fund" is exhausted, the pressure may be expected to be revealed, at least in part, in increases in the national debt.

One of the most direct, though least known, pressures to inflation is government obligations contracted by serving as guarantor of mortgages. The best known of these guarantees are the VA and FHA guarantees. The U. S. government guarantees up to 20 percent of VA loans, a guarantee which enables veterans to buy houses with no down payment, if they can otherwise meet the requirements of a lender. The FHA insures loans on which the house buyer may make as little as a 5 percent down payment. There are a considerable variety of other government guarantee programs in real estate, but enough has been told to show the principle of guarantee underlying and making the government obligations.

Such guarantees as these tilt government toward inflationary policies. It is generally claimed that VA and FHA loans have been successful in that losses have been small. There is not much mystery as to why this should have been so. Impractical programs have been saved from their predictable consequences by long-term inflation. It has worked in two ways to do this. One is that wages have generally risen over the years, making it easier for the mortgagor to make his payments. The other is that any house tolerably well taken care of over the last twenty or thirty years has appreciated in dollar value, other things being equal. This has meant that the owner could usually sell it for more than was owed on it, however much that might be, or, if foreclosure did take place, the amount of the mortgaged indebtedness would probably be recovered. The real guarantor of the mortgages, then, has usually been inflation.

It might be supposed that the government obligations on mortgages are limited to the extent of the guarantees. This is only superficially the case, however. Government obligations extend to cover a large portion of the mortgaged indebtedness in the United States. They do so because the federal government guarantees most of the deposits in banks and savings institutions by the Federal Deposit Insurance Corporation and the Federal Savings and Loan Insurance Corporation. In turn, mortgages constitute a large portion of the assets of banks and savings institutions. It is reasonable to suppose, then, that if governments had to pay off depositors and savers they would, in effect, be making good on these loans. Continuing inflation enables banks to operate with relatively small reserves, particularly when the very mode of inflation is the monetizing of debt.

Government Guarantees

The total obligations of the U. S. government include both formal and tacit or informal obligations. The government underwrites more kinds of undertakings than the present writer knows or could describe if he did. A vast assortment of projects proceed on the basis of such underwritten guarantees. Beyond these, the government has thus far shown a willingness to shore up any failing business, city, or government. The loans to Lockheed, the aid to eastern railroads, the subsidizing of AMTRAK, illustrate the government's role in business. The recent bailing out of New York City shows the possibilities of government action in the area of local government.

How can the federal government act as guarantor for and come to the rescue of all these people and institutions? Is it because the federal government is so well managed and has so many resources upon which to call? Not basically. The federal government's finances have been no better managed, if anything they have been worse managed, than Lockheed or Penn Central or New York City. It is sometimes alleged that the federal government is an efficient taxer and has a much better base for taxes than state or local governments. This may or may not be true, in theory, but in fact for many years running now it has spent more than it has taken in by way of taxes. In short, the claim if correct is nonetheless irrelevant. The *difference* between the federal government and these private businesses and other governments lies in the *power to inflate,* the power to increase the money supply by monetizing its debt. The vast obligations of the federal government are "secured" by the debt itself. These obligations are the potential of mounting waves which could destroy our money supply even as they wiped out the indebtedness.

Political Pressures

There are other pressures to inflation than those that arise directly from obligations of the government. They are what may be called *political* pressures. Some of these pressures evince themselves in the desire of politicians to spend while avoiding the onus of taxing to get the money, or all of it. There is a *multiplier* effect to this kind of government spending, though not in the sense in which some economists use the word. By raising less by taxes than is spent, by making up the difference with fiat, i.e., printing press, money, the government puts more into circulation than it takes out. The initial impact of this additional money, if it is not entirely discounted, is to spur investment and all sorts of risk taking. An aura of prosperity quite often accompanies the spurts of new money. In the long run, whatever time it takes for the untoward effects of inflation to take place, the aura of prosperity dissipates as prices rise, wages lag, and malinvestments induced by false signals sent into the market produce their inevitable crop of failures. The long runs grow shorter and shorter, too, with successive spurts of inflation, for people come more and more to expect that the aura of prosperity is only an aura. The stock market, for example, can remain bearish through a whole series of spurts of inflation.

There are, then, two rather direct political pressures to inflation. One is for politicians to be able to spend and avoid the responsibility for new taxes. The other is to create the aura of prosperity at crucial times. Presidents have come to depend on this inflation-induced aura of prosperity in the months just before a presidential election. If the President is a candidate himself, he will press to do it in his own behalf. If not, he may be expected to try to do it on behalf of his party. It might be supposed that the members of Congress of the party out of power would want to thwart this effort, but it does not follow. Their re-election may be dependent also upon the appearance of prosperity. It may well be that the greatest danger of a runaway inflation arises from the political necessity for prosperity in an election year when it is coupled with mounting popular resistance to accept the false signals sent into the market by inflation. The pressure is there to pour more and more money into circulation to achieve the desired result. This tide of inflation could knock sufficient holes in the dikes to allow the whole sea of claims on government to sweep through and destroy the money.

Hikes in Minimum Wage

Congress and the President reap political gains in yet another way that depends on inflation. They periodically raise the minimum wage, increase the pay of government employees, give raises to those on pensions, such as retired military personnel, and so forth. Not only is inflation sometimes named as the reason for these increases but it also makes them possible. Without the inflation, there would not be these rounds of increases which members of Congress particularly call attention to in order to claim credit from some of their constituents.

Labor unions contribute considerably to the pressure for inflation. To keep its following, the union finds it expedient to demand and get higher wages in each successive contract. Union officers seek also to maintain and even increase union membership because their salaries depend upon the number paying and amount of the dues and the effectiveness of the union is tied to its financial resources in a variety of ways.

These two goals—perennial money-wage increases and stable or increasing union membership—are incompatible in the short run and impossible in the long run, except under one condition, a regular and continuing expansion of the money supply. All other means of accomplishing this are strictly limited in their application, and self-defeating when employed over an extended period of time. (Indeed, inflation is self-defeating also, but not so obviously or directly.) For example, it is often alleged that wages could be increased by giving workers a larger proportion of the gross income of a company. But this could not continue year after year indefinitely, for there is only 100 percent, and eventually wages would take all the income. Long before that occurred, however, the company would have been driven out of business, and union membership reduced by the number disemployed. For an industry as a whole, the process would be less dramatic. The price of the product or service would be increased to cover the higher wage costs or machines would replace workers. In any case, the number of workers, i.e., union members, would decline. Another device that allegedly could result in money-wage increases would be increased productivity. But overall increases in productivity will not result in money wage increases, in the absence of an increase in the money supply; the result, given competition, will be a reduction in prices of product or service. Lower prices would increase the *real* wages of workmen, but unions could hardly claim credit for the increase, since money wages would remain the same, or might even decline.

In sum, unions depend on inflation for their growth, and, with some few possible exceptions, even their survival. The periods of dramatic union growth—World War I, the 1930s, World War II and after—have been periods of inflation. The only extended period of continued large-scale union membership in our history has been one of a continued and long-term increase of the money supply, namely from the 1930s to the present.

A Fearsome Burden of Debt

There are, then, a host of pressures toward continued and mounting inflation. Some estimate that the total obligations of the government now amount to something like $5 trillion. If that figure was correct yesterday, it has probably already been surpassed now, and will continue to grow larger if the government persists in contracting more and more obligations. The obligations of the government are such that if all of them had to be met that could only be done by such a massive inflation that the value of our money would be destroyed. Not only that, but if the government had to pay off on all that it has underwritten, it would surely become receiver for the banks, savings and loan associations, many industries, and a considerable portion of the homes and landed estates in the country. These "guarantees" are backed by debt; they are potential massive pressures to inflation, and the present means for meeting the obligations is the monetizing of debt.

There should be no doubt, then, that the government is on a course that if followed will destroy the money, may result in government's becoming receiver for increasingly large amounts of property, and will almost inevitably lead to loss of faith in the government. Someone looking at this from another planet or an enemy country might view all this with equanimity, or even with glee. After all, they might say, the government has made its bed, let it lie in it. Those of us who live in the country, who would not know where to go to find better circumstance if we would, must perforce view the matter differently. The government may have made the bed, but all of us are going to lie in it. If there is some way to avert the collision between money supply and obligations, some way to reverse our course without, say, ruinous deflation, we would wish to find it.

There are some things that should be done. They should be done because they are in the right direction and because they offer some prospect of working. It needs to be clear however, that in offering them the present writer is steering as clear of detailed monetary theory as he can. He is not going to say what should back our money, how much reserves banks should have against deposits, who should issue the currency, or any other of hundreds of questions that could be raised. His predilection is to have as many of these questions answered in the market as possible, but even that is put aside somewhat here in order to stick as close as possible to some general principle. The reasons for these limitations should become apparent in what follows.

No Drastic Changes

Whatever the remedy for the situation there may be, there is one thing it should not be. It should not be drastic. Whatever is done will affect established institutions, contracts, wages, prices, and a whole complex of delicate relationships. The least direct and immediate effect there is on any of these the better. Nor should the action taken excite unnecessary fears about the possible consequences. For these reasons, only so much should be done as produces the desired change of direction.

Two things only need to be done. They are interrelated in that the first will almost certainly lead to the second. The first is to stabilize the money supply. A stable money supply need not be and probably could not be a static money supply. It only means that the pressures to the increase of it be counterbalanced by pressures to decrease it. This is what is meant by or produces stability in any thing. The second is to build in pressures toward fiscal responsibility by the government (and individuals, and companies, and banks, too), toward the reduction of debt, toward balanced budgets, toward reduction of government obligations, and toward the disentanglement of government from the economy.

Some have apparently hoped that political pressures could be built up to counterbalance the thrusts to inflation. This hope probably underlies at least some of the effort to inform the public that government's increasing of the money supply is at the root of inflation or what is causing it. It is a forlorn hope. If everyone in the country, including small children, knew that inflation is the increase of the money supply and that government is the villain of the piece, my guess is that the political pressures would not be significantly altered. The reason is not far to seek. *The only ones hurt by inflation are all of us,* though admittedly some are hurt worse than others, at least in the intermediate stages of it. Hence, the resistance to inflation is vague, general, and diffuse, apt to be relegated to the realm of hankerings for a good five-cent cigar. By contrast, the benefits of inflation are particular, immediate, and accrue to those in the seats of power, i.e., politicians. All of us wish that the prices others charge would be stable or even decline, but each of us wants even more to get more for what we sell. Inflation feeds on the lure that we can do this, though it is almost entirely an illusion.

Remove Monetary Powers

There is little likelihood, then, that political pressures can ever be built up that will counter the built-in tilt toward inflation. This is just another way of saying that government cannot be trusted with the power to manage the money supply. That is not surprising, after all. No one of us could be trusted with such power. If one of us is multiplied by 500, or 5,000, he does not thereby become more trustworthy, though he may well become more devious. Give any man, or group of men, control of the money supply, couple it with the possibility that he can benefit by increasing it, and the question becomes not whether he will do it but when. Each of us has enough "Après moi, le déluge" not to be deterred from acts simply because they will have some dire consequence in the uncertain future.

What needs to be done, then, is to divest the federal government of its power to increase or decrease the money supply. The expansible and contractible portion of the money supply today consists of the outstanding currency plus demand deposits in banks less the reserves held against the deposits. The money supply can be increased by increasing debts, both those of the federal government and private debts. The government manipulates this or controls it by setting reserve requirements for banks and by the sale or buying of securities by the Federal Reserve banks. Since there is no real limit to indebtedness, the only limit to the money supply is the reserve requirement, but it can be lowered virtually at will. Our money is money by the decree of the government—fiat money— separated from this only by the backing it receives from the debt.

Two changes in the system would set up major and probably sufficient counter pressures to inflation. They are changes of a character that most people would hardly notice. One would be to prohibit the monetizing of debt, both public and private. It should never have been permitted in the first place. Debt is no security for anything, least of all money. It is fraudulent to pass off as money what is secured only by debt. The most effective way to accomplish this prohibition would be by constitutional amendment.

Reserve Requirements

The second change would be in the reserve requirements. There are, it has been noted, two ways that money is created: by printing currency and by creating demand deposits in banks. If debt could not be monetized, there might still be a way for government to manipulate the money by altering reserve requirements. The device involved is called fractional reserve banking. Two varieties of fractional reserve have been practiced historically. One is the reserve against the currency. When currency was backed by and convertible into gold, banks of issue usually had a reserve in gold against their outstanding currency, a reserve which was only some portion of the total—a "fraction" of it. This practice of having fractional reserves against the currency has been continued, though today it means little by way of restraint. The other kind of fractional reserve is the reserves in cash which a commercial bank holds against deposits. Both varieties of fractional reserve can be and are used to increase the money supply.

There is nothing wrong, *per se,* with operating on fractional reserve. It is an old and reasonably honorable practice. Banks are not the only institutions which keep on hand only a fraction of the amount needed to pay off all their obligations, if they should have to do so all at once. So do savings institutions, insurance companies, furniture stores, appliance dealers, and companies of every sort and description. Hardly an individual could be found who has the cash on hand to meet his forthcoming obligations. He expects to pay them out of income as they come due, keeping on hand only sufficient cash for emergencies, if he is prudent. Banks do likewise, though admittedly much of their "income" consists of deposits by their customers.

At any rate, fractional reserve in general is not at issue here. What is properly at issue is any fractional reserve held against the money supply. There is no excuse for a fractional reserve against the money supply. Money should be backed by a 100 percent reserve of what is used to back it. Anything less is fraudulent and should be punished the same as any other fraud. Any reserve of less than 100 percent amounts to a false claim as to the character of the money issued. Currency, then, should be backed by 100 percent reserves against it. If those reserves cannot be debt, they must consist of some sort of assets, assets whose value could be determined in the marketplace and which, if they had to be produced, would equal in value the currency issued against them.

Bank deposits can be held in check and limited by requiring that there be in reserve against them either cash or collateral in the amount of 100 percent or better. The effect of this should be that banks could only create a deposit on an unsecured loan—debt—by increasing their cash reserves in an amount equal to it. This would not prevent some fluctuation in the money supply, but it would create pressures to hold the supply in check.

How would government service its debt if it could not do so by monetizing it? It could do so in the same way other organizations and individuals service theirs, namely, by borrowing from willing lenders who will lend on unsecured notes or by putting up sufficient collateral to secure the loans. Since banks would have little inducement to grant unsecured loans, such loans as government could obtain without security would be uninflationary. If government put up collateral, such as national forests, this could result in some increase of the money supply, but there would be inherent limits to and checks upon it.

In short, if government could not monetize the debt or manipulate the reserve requirements, the counter pressures to inflation would be developed. Government would either have to raise the moneys it spent by taxes or by divesting itself of its assets. The pressure would be on to reduce the debt. The pressure would be on to reduce obligations. Government would have very little incentive to increase its obligations and strong motives to reduce them. Every pressure to inflation, both public and private, would be matched or counterbalanced by pressures to reduce and pay off debts. There is no reason why these two changes should be strongly inflationary or deflationary. All the money in circulation could remain there provided only that backing were found for it. All debts and obligations would stand as they had been, counterbalanced only by a pressure to reduce and pay them off. Government would no longer control the money supply; it would, instead, be held in check by it.

The Rotting Fabric of Trust

by Donald L. Kemmerer

As we drove from New Delhi to Agra to see India's famous Taj Mahal, we passed through extremely primitive villages. There was not a petrol can, broken umbrella, or empty bottle to be seen. We thought, "Perhaps a Time Machine has carried us back 1,000 years or more." In one dusty hamlet we saw an Indian woman wearing a crude anklet of silver. The reason for this abysmal squalor struck us. That silver was all her savings and no one was going to take it from her. She didn't trust her neighbors and they didn't trust anyone either. There could be no banks, and businessmen found it almost impossible to borrow. Progress was at a standstill and had been for centuries because an all-important ingredient was missing in that economy, the fabric of trust between men, that enables them to work together willingly toward productive ends.

When men work with tools and equipment—economists call these capital—they can produce more than when they work with bare hands. But to produce capital it takes a willingness to save and to invest those savings. And men will save little and invest less unless they trust their fellow men as individuals and believe that their property and savings will be safe and that the money of the realm will hold its buying power. These are the warp and woof of the fabric of trust.

Aggravated Inflation

In the United States today, due to government-caused expansion of the supply of money and credit, inflation is raging at a rate of about 13 percent a year, double what it was two years ago. If this continues, the dollar will lose half of its present buying power in six years. That present buying power is only a fifth of what it was in 1933. Those conditions are not conducive to saving. The rate of saving and of capital investment is

Dr. Kemmerer, former president of The Committee for Monetary Research and Education, Inc., taught economic history for many years at the University of Illinois. This article first appeared in *The Freeman*, March 1980.

five percent a year, the lowest among major modern nations.

Such misuse of power by government sets a bad example to many who then lash back at government and often at others too. The government should set an example of trustworthiness. Its courts punish counterfeiters, embezzlers, and thieves. To find the government itself engaged in similar actions is demoralizing. A government that inflates and destroys the buying power of its money pours, as it were, a destructive acid over the economy's fabric of trust which rots the fabric and seriously damages the economy.

Just how suspicious Americans are of their government's money can be seen by the fact that millions of them are putting more and more of the savings they have left into gold, silver, diamonds, rare coins, stamps, paintings, and antique furniture, to name just some items. All of these they increasingly look upon as preferable to banking their money, the buying power of which melts away like an ice cube in July. The degree of distrust can be gauged by the fact that the prices of these non-income producing "stores of value" have been bid up much higher than wholesale or consumer price levels have risen. Whereas price levels today are five times higher than in 1933, the price of gold is 29 times higher, of silver at least 70 times and of precious gems 20 to 60 times higher. These prices rise out of distrust and fear more than they do from speculation.

Inflation is rotting away the fabric of trust which helped so much to make this nation economically strong. Fear is rendering a growing portion of our savings as unproductive as that Indian woman's anklet. President Jimmy Carter has said we must lower our standard of living. He and Congress, and preceding administrations, too, by their inflationary policies, have been bringing on that lowering process for some time. Let us hope that we never regress to conditions in those Indian villages, but we are headed in that direction. That precious fabric of trust is disintegrating before our eyes.

Dishonest About Inflation

by Melvin D. Barger

Most of the opinion polls tell us that inflation is the public's Number
One worry. We shouldn't need the pollsters to tell us that. We can listen to
the complaints in the lines at the supermarkets, read the headlines in news-
papers, or hear the pronouncements of business leaders and political can-
didates. Inflation is a terrible cancer that must be brought under control,
we are constantly warned, or we face a bleak future and perhaps an economic disaster.

But what *causes* inflation? Many economists and savants tell us that
inflation is a very complex problem with neither a single cause nor a
single solution. Few economists would dare deny that arbitrary government
expansion of money and credit produces inflation. Yet, there seems to be
a universal desire to bring in other alleged causes: the greed of unions and
businessmen, government regulations, rising oil prices, and even such
matters as lowered American productivity and reduced capital investment.

What is behind all this confusion about inflation? It grows out of the
same character defect that causes inflation in the first place. That character defect is *dishonesty,* and it has seduced a whole nation. But events
may eventually force us to accept inflation as a *dishonest human action*
that can be avoided if people have the will and the understanding to do so.
Nor is inflation a complex problem when one is prepared to see it as a
moral issue rather than simply as political or social phenomena.

A steel company executive named Enders M. Voorhees pointed to the
moral problem of inflation in a 1950 speech entitled "Wanted—Dependable Dollars." Even then, corporate financial officers in Mr. Voorhees'
position were discovering that inflation distorted business calculations
and made future business planning a nightmare. In the same speech, he
unashamedly showed a preference for the terms "dependable dollars" or
"honest money" rather than such terms as "sound money" or "gold stan-

Mr. Barger is a retired corporate public relations executive and writer who lives in Toledo, Ohio.
This article is reprinted from the December 1979 issue of *The Freeman.*

dard." He had harsh words for "printing-press money," i.e., money created by government manipulations. But why were we beguiled by "printing press" money and why were we unable to stop inflation? Mr. Voorhees
concluded, "In the end we may discover that it is *our own deficiency in
moral stamina* that is to blame, and that the printing-press operators are
merely reflecting our own attitudes" (emphasis added).[1]

Mr. Voorhees was politely saying that character defects get in the
way of efforts to stop inflation. He could have gone on to say that dishonest money is produced by dishonest people who are trapped by greed,
fear, and weakness. This would be a very strong statement, but the facts
bear it out. Inflation begins with an expansion of the money supply which
immediately produces benefits for certain people while causing losses for
others. In general, people on fixed incomes and holders of bonds, loans,
and savings accounts are cheated, while borrowers, property owners, and
inflation-wise speculators show gains.

Lying and Cheating

Lying and bland promises are an essential part of the inflation program. The public is constantly told that inflation will be brought under
control, for it is important that most of the victims be unaware of what is
going on. Still, a student of inflation is finally forced to believe that the
public wants to go on believing in the inflation game. The old saying,
"You can't cheat an honest man," may have some relevance to the way we
are cheating and being cheated by inflation.

It would be unfair to say that the current generation of Americans is
less honest than earlier generations that somehow were able to maintain
an "honest" or "dependable" dollar. And for that matter, it would even be
unfair to say that Americans are more dishonest, say, than the Germans or
Swiss who have been able to maintain the strength of their currencies.
Our problem, as Americans, is that we have been practicing a *selective
dishonesty*. While often insisting on rigorous honesty in other matters, we
have accepted the dishonest practices that produce inflation. Then we
have gone further in this deceit and have attributed the shrinkage of the
dollar's buying power to conditions that are really the *effects* of inflating.
This tends to deflect attention from the actions that dilute the market value
of money and ought to be stopped.

Needed: An Acceptable Definition

One of our most disturbing problems is that professional economists do not agree in their definitions of inflation. One of the most widely accepted definitions of inflation is that it is a rising general level of prices.[2] Another popular definition of inflation is "too much money chasing too few goods." Actually, more honest and precise than either of these definitions would be an explanation of the actions that cause prices to rise *generally* or bring "too much money" into existence.

The public should understand that a widespread drought may result in temporarily higher prices for food, relative to prices of other things. But that is not the same as a government action that arbitrarily produces more paper money and credit and results in a persisting general increase in prices.

Why do professional economists employ such deceptive and misleading definitions of a condition that could prove to be a terminal illness for our way of life? One reason for this dishonesty is that the need to maintain "sound" or "honest" money was badly ridiculed and discredited in the early 1930s and since then has never been defended except by a few economists. There is also something about inflation that promotes demands for centralized government control, which many economists advocate. Finally, the Keynesian deficit spending programs endorsed by many economists make inflation unavoidable.

Yet another argument against "honest money" is that it is a return to the gold standard, which had its severe critics and was often looked upon as a means of keeping money scarce and concentrating power in the hands of eastern bankers. Actually, honest money could take several forms and could be backed by metals and commodities other than gold. It is even possible to conceive of a privately issued currency without any specific backing other than the assets of the bank or company which offers it. A gold standard will soon collapse if it is seen as a hindrance to progress rather than a way of protecting the public.

Effects Seen as Causes

In the general dishonesty about inflation, most experts make the error of blaming inflation on conditions that are really the *effects* of expanding the money supply. Business leaders like to focus on "cost-push" inflation, for example, with unions as the villains. According to this argument, monopolistic unions are able to impose increased costs on business which must eventually be passed through as price increases. If unions would only be less greedy, cost-push inflation could be kept under control.

Union leaders and their staff economists seize on the same argument, usually with the twist that inflation is caused by unwarranted price increases, excessive profits, high executive salaries, and monopolistic or oligopolistic enterprises. Both unions and management, in making such arguments, play directly into the hands of politicians who would like to institute wage-price controls. Despite the fact that wage-price controls are virtually unworkable and result in a bureaucratic nightmare, the demand for them is kept alive by the persistent belief that unions cause inflation by raising wages or managements cause the same condition by increasing prices.

Professional economists could perform a great service by rooting out the fallacies in these beliefs. They could show, for example, that raising either wages or prices without corresponding expansion of the money supply will result in unemployment; there is less demand for either labor or goods if wages and prices go up with no equivalent increase in available money. With no expansion in the money supply, workers who demand too much or businesses which raise prices above the market would merely lose out to competitors.

Blaming Government Regulations

Inflation commentators have recently discovered another culprit in producing inflation: the high costs of government regulation. This has been useful to managements protesting the costs of meeting factory emission regulations or of making government-required product changes. There are good reasons to oppose these regulations and to deplore the costs of meeting them. It is false, however, to say that costly government regulations *cause* inflation.

The economic effect of a government regulation is exactly the same as a wage increase or any other cost, including higher oil prices. It is something that must be included in the prices of the goods or services being offered by the company. Taxes are in the same category. And if the firm's customers will not accept the increased prices, the company either will go out of business or will divert its production to lines that can be marketed profitably.

But regulations in themselves do not cause inflation. They do cause higher prices of certain products. These higher prices are mistakenly called inflationary, when they really reflect higher costs. The customer who must pay these higher prices will make equivalent reductions in other purchases.

Is Low Productivity a Cause of Inflation?

Low productivity is still another suspect in causing the inflation mess. With lower-priced imports flooding the country, there is increased concern about conditions that adversely affect American productivity. One of these conditions is the high cost of wages and benefits which raises unit costs of American goods. There is also deepening concern about the decline in capital investments. It is alleged that our own plant capacity is becoming obsolete and inefficient in comparison with the plants of foreign producers. Meanwhile, prices of most manufactured goods are going up. But with higher productivity, prices would tend to stabilize, or at least the increases would not be so large.

Here again, low productivity is blamed because it supposedly increases the unit costs of certain products. Productivity itself has nothing to do with causing inflation, nor can it stop the process. The best spur to productivity is the producer's desire to capture a larger share of the market and to increase his overall productivity. Few producers are likely to increase their efforts simply to fight inflation.

But there is a very serious deception in the effort to use higher productivity as an inflation-fighter. This deception comes from defining inflation as a general rise in prices. Theoretically, an annual increase of four percent in the money supply would not result in a general price rise if there also was a four percent improvement in productivity. Prices would probably remain at the same level.

This would not mean, however, that inflation had been stopped. It would only mean that its effects had been concealed. For, without an arbitrary expansion of the money supply, the four percent improvement in productivity would have gone to certain workers, owners, and customers, as wages, dividends, or lower prices. So increased productivity only makes inflation less visible, and perhaps more acceptable politically. But it is not the answer to inflation.

The End of Dishonesty

We can probably expect more dishonesty about inflation until events force us to change our ways. There is reason to believe that the American people become very worried when inflation passes the double-digit level. While this does not lead to a complete understanding of the problem, it does cast doubt on some of the glib explanations and solutions being offered. Unfortunately, the most recent surge in inflation was attributed to higher oil prices, when in reality the OPEC nations who raise their crude prices do so to protect themselves from the continuous inflating of the American dollar.

Yet, honesty or truth about money must always have its day; even the inflationists know that. As Ludwig von Mises explained, inflation cannot go on endlessly. "If one does not stop in time the pernicious policy of increasing the quantity of money and fiduciary media, the nation's currency system collapses entirely. The monetary unit's purchasing power sinks to a point which for all practical purposes is not better than zero." Still, Mises believed that money and credit expansion could be stopped in time if people had only the will and the understanding to do so.[3]

Hans F. Sennholz, an economist who studied under Mises, has been less optimistic about the future of the dollar. In his view, two-digit inflation will be ended only by the advent of three-digit inflation. He also has suggested that American inflation may end in a frenzied, hysterical spending debacle not unlike that which overtook Germany in 1923. But whether the landing from dishonest money is soft or hard, Americans will some day become more honest about the causes and effects of inflation. We will become courageous enough to demand honest, or dependable, money.

And we should not be too hard on ourselves when we finally learn how we have been deceived about the nature of inflation. Mr. Voorhees, in his plea for dependable dollars, pointed out that it seems to be those people who have had bitter personal experience of living under bad currencies who most appreciate good currencies and are willing to make some sacrifices to secure and maintain them. He was probably referring to the West Germans, whose bitter experiences of 1923 probably taught them the value of strong, honest, dependable, money.

We have had no experience similar to Germany's runaway inflation of 1923. Let's hope we don't have to endure such a disaster, which some observers thought was a worse calamity for Germany than their losses of

World War I. But adversity, if it cannot be avoided, can at least be put to good use. In the case of an inflationary collapse, it could teach us honesty. As Sennholz says, "Affliction is a school of virtue that may correct levity and interrupt the confidence of sinning. But how long and how often must man be afflicted before he learns the lesson?"[4]

---

1. See Enders M. Voorhees, *Financial Policy in a Changing Economy* (Lebanon, Pa.: Sowers Printing Company, 1970). See particularly pp. 184-200. This speech was presented at Dartmouth in 1950.

2. Campbell R. McConnell, *Economics* (New York: McGraw-Hill. 1975), p. 197.

3. Ludwig von Mises, *Planning for Freedom* (South Holland, Ill.: Libertarian Press, 1974), p. 155.

4. Hans F. Sennholz "Two-Digit Inflation," *The Freeman,* January 1975.

Blaming the Victims: The Government's Theory of Inflation

by Robert Higgs

In October, 1978, President Jimmy Carter announced an elaborate program of wage-price guidelines to serve as the keystone of his administration's anti-inflation policies. What makes the President's advisers believe that the sword of guidelines can slay the dragon of inflation? Like other knights-errant, they are convinced that they understand the anatomy of the beast, that they know just where they must drive their lance in order to kill or at least disable it. Putting metaphors aside, I am saying that they have a theory about the nature and causes of inflation that suggests guidelines can be an effective anti-inflation policy. It is not a very coherent or well articulated theory, but its main elements can be discerned fairly readily in the statements emanating from the President himself, from the Council on Wage and Price Stability (COWPS), and from the Council of Economic Advisers (CEA).

The Official Line

The fundamental assumption of the government's theory is that competitive market forces have little or nothing to do with the determination of prices and wages. "The pay and price standards," the President's advisers say, "are designed to be guides for decision-making agents who have *discretionary power* in wage and price determination."[1] They believe, in other words, that firms can set whatever prices they want and, in conjunction with the unions, whatever wages they want.

Alfred Kahn, the chairman of COWPS, and his fellow enforcers obviously believe that this discretionary power resides especially within the largest corporations and labor unions, for those institutions have been the focus of their monitoring efforts from the very beginning. The notion that

---

Dr. Higgs is a noted writer and a popular lecturer on economic and monetary affairs. This article is reprinted from *The Freeman*, July 1979.

large firms and unions possess significant power to resist competitive market pressures is known to economists as the administered-price theory. The President's men clearly embrace this theory root and branch.

From the administered price theory of price and wage determination, it is but a short step to the cost-push theory of inflation. The government economists have taken this step. In this year's Report of the Council of Economic Advisers, one finds repeated assertions that during the current expansion the economy, even in 1978, has not yet experienced excessive aggregate demand for its output. Idle plant and labor, it is said, have been ample to accommodate increases in the economy's rate of output.[2] Rather than the pressure of excess demand driving up prices, the government economists see cost increases, particularly increased costs of labor, pushing prices up. "[T]he rise in unit labor costs," it is alleged, was "a major factor in the acceleration of inflation" in 1978.[3]

By combining the assumption of discretionary market power, the administered-price theory, and the cost-push theory of inflation, the government economists arrive at the concept of a *wage-price spiral* as a characterization of the causal structure of inflation. In this view, large firms and unions conspire to push up wages excessively; the firms then pass the increased labor costs along to final consumers and other purchasers in the form of higher product prices, thereby creating inflation. In response to this inflation, which reduces real wages, the unions subsequently return to the bargaining tables with even more outrageous demands. The economy is propelled through successive rounds of inflation kept in motion by the powerful but socially irresponsible actions of the large companies and unions. The rest of the economy, with its smaller firms and mostly nonunionized workers, falls passively into line with the patterns set by the large firms and unions.

The wage-price spiral is the government's accepted view of the basic inflationary process, but the President's men complement this basic conception with two auxiliary theories of inflation: the exogenous shock theory and the self-sustaining expectations theory.

The exogenous shock theory has been especially popular of late. In his economic report to the Congress this year, the President relied on it almost exclusively to explain the recent increase in the rate of inflation. Mr. Carter identified several important shocks:

> *Cold winter weather* affected food supplies and prices. *Depreciation of the dollar* in foreign exchange markets added to prices of imports and to prices of goods produced by U.S. firms that compete with imported products. Costs of land and building materials were driven up by *exuberant demands for new homes,* and the *rise of mortgage interest rates* added to the costs of buying a home. At the same time, the cumulative effects of *government legislation and regulation* over recent years gave further impetus to cost pressures. A large part of the worsening of inflation last year, however, stemmed from *poor productivity.*[4]

Of course, the most frequently cited exogenous shock of all is the effect on fuel and related prices when the OPEC cartel raises the price of oil. All of these exogenous shocks are thought to be external to the normal functioning of the American economy but additive to its allegedly inherent wage-price spiral. They are seen as unfortunate accidents—our luck seems always to be bad—that make inflation even worse than it would be as a result of the internal wage-price spiral.

Finally, the self-sustaining expectations theory completes the government's overall conception of the inflationary process by suggesting that, once inflation has gone on for a while, people expect it to continue; and these expectations, all by themselves, can then continue to push prices up year after year. In the words of the CEA, "Once under way, a high rate of inflation generates responses and adaptations by individuals and institutions that *perpetuate the wage-price spiral,* even in periods of economic slack. . . . The formal and informal adaptations to a longstanding inflation exert a powerful force tending to sustain inflation *even after the originating causes have disappeared.* "[5] Those who regard economics as the dismal science will certainly find ample confirmation in this theory.

Fallacies of the Official Line

Unfortunately, the entire edifice of the government's theories—the assumption of discretionary power, the administered-price theory, the wage-price spiral, the exogenous shocks, the self-sustaining expectation—all of it is the rankest nonsense as an explanation of inflation. There are a variety of pertinent reasons for rejecting the official line.

Consider for a moment the assumption of discretionary power. This unfortunate belief seems to have grown out of the common observation that many firms can increase their prices somewhat without losing *all* their sales. What the notion of discretionary power neglects, however, is that, unless the demand for its product has increased, a firm that raises its prices will experience a reduction in unit sales volume. Even the true monopolist, the single seller with the market all to himself, must contend with the law of demand and, of course, true monopolists are as rare as hen's teeth. Clearly, even firms in highly concentrated industries must, and do, compete for the customer's favor. Despite what Professor J. K. Galbraith and a host of lesser known polemicists have asserted, it simply is not true that large firms can raise their prices at will without suffering any consequent reductions in sales. Even if this ever had been the case, we can be confident that business managers would long since have taken advantage of such a marvelous opportunity for adding effortlessly to their profits. The idea that large firms possess bottomless reservoirs of discretionary pricing power is preposterous in its logic and without any basis in fact.

The closely related theory of administered pricing is similarly flawed. George Stigler and James Kindahl, in the most painstaking and carefully designed study of industrial prices ever conducted, found that industrial markets, including those with only a few large firms, are *not* "unresponsive in their pricing to changes in general business conditions";[8] that is, the price data refute the administered-price theory.

Economists have also tested the relationship between industrial concentration and the rate of price increase among industries. Both in the late 1960s and in the decade terminating in 1977, they have found that the correlation between concentration and price increases is *negative;* that is, the industries with a few large firms have had *smaller* average increases in prices than the industries with many small firms.[7]

George Shultz, the former Secretary of the Treasury who occupied an important administrative position during the period of President Nixon's price controls, has pointed out that between 1971 and 1974 prices rose most rapidly in sectors with many small firms (e.g., agriculture), in sectors dominated by the government (e.g., health services), and in sectors heavily involved in international trade (e.g., petroleum).[8]

One can draw similar conclusions for the past 11 years by examining the broad components of the consumer price index: since 1967 (index = 100), the greatest increases have occurred in the prices of home ownership (238.8) and medical care (227.0), both sectors that are dominated by a multitude of small suppliers. Even increased fuel and utilities prices (218.5), which have been so profoundly affected by the actions of the OPEC cartel, have barely equaled the increased prices of food (217.8), which is supplied by tens of thousands of stores and middlemen and millions of farmers.[9]

The administered-price theory, scientifically speaking, is a joke—though not a very funny one. Nevertheless, it is very popular among the general public, who are infected with a chronic distrust of big business' motives and actions. And it is, if anything, even more cherished by politicians. As Shultz has said, "The politician knows the political mileage to be gained by pushing around the big boys in the economy, whether or not it makes any economic sense."[10]

Without the assumption of discretionary power and the administered-price theory to support them, the cost-push theory of inflation and the notion of a wage-price spiral collapse of their own weight.

Inflation versus Relative Price Changes

In any event, the cost-push theory, along with the exogenous shock theory, fundamentally misconstrues the issue in question. Inflation is *a persistent, ongoing increase in the average price of the economy's total output;* or, looking at it from its other side, inflation is a persistent, ongoing decline in the average purchasing power of money. Unfortunately, it has become commonplace for people to refer to any increase in the money price of a particular product, no matter how small or how transitory, as inflationary. This confuses the price of a particular good with the average price of all goods. It is extremely important to understand that in *any real economy some increases in the prices of particular goods would necessarily occur even if the overall price level were perfectly stable.* Obviously, such particular price increases would change only the *relative* prices of particular goods; declines in other individual prices would offset these increases, thereby keeping the aggregate price level constant.

The fallacies of the cost-push theory can be illustrated well by a simple, hypothetical example. Suppose a firm and a union enter into a conspiracy to raise the wage paid to the firm's workers far above the competitive level; the firm then raises the price of its product enough to offset the increased labor costs; but the total volume of money expenditures in the overall economy remains the same. What will happen?

Under these circumstances, the firm will find that because the relative price of its product has increased, it will be unable to sell as much of its output as before; it will have to reduce production and lay off workers. These workers must go elsewhere to obtain employment. The increased supply of workers elsewhere will tend to reduce the wage rate, lower production costs, and encourage enlarged production and therefore reduced product prices elsewhere. The ultimate outcome of these readjustments is that the conspiring firm to some extent prices itself out of the market; its labor force shrinks, and some of its initial workers find work elsewhere at lower wages. The price of the firm's product does increase, to be sure, but prices elsewhere decrease. Inflation, most emphatically, does not occur.

The truth is that as long as the aggregate volume of money expenditures is held fixed, cost increases in particular firms or sectors, no matter what their origin, can cause only *relative price* changes. Such cost increases alone *cannot* cause inflation, which is a persistent, ongoing increase in the *average* price of *all* goods and services.

Recall the alleged causes of increased inflation in 1978 as identified by President Carter. They include bad weather, dollar depreciation against foreign currencies, increased demand for housing, and higher mortgage interest rates. Each of these can cause a change in relative prices, but none of them can cause inflation. The cost-push theory of inflation, from an intellectual standpoint, is simply indefensible. It remains immensely useful for politicians, however, because it shifts the blame for inflation onto the private sector. But private citizens cannot cause inflation, because they cannot regulate the volume of aggregate money expenditure. Whoever controls that bears the blame for inflation and holds the only key to stopping it.

What Really Causes Inflation?

Inflation occurs, by definition, when the economy's aggregate volume of money expenditure grows faster than its aggregate real output. The excessive growth of money expenditures can have, again by definition, only two sources: either the velocity of monetary circulation grows excessively or the money stock itself grows excessively (or both). Our current inflation is attributable almost entirely to excessive growth of the money stock.

Because the excessive growth of the money stock and the inflation it causes do not happen simultaneously, some people always fail to perceive the relationship. Increases in the money stock take some time before their effect on the volume of expenditure becomes significant. But once the actual lag is recognized, the relationship is seen to be very close. By relating the rate of inflation in a given year to the average rate of growth of the broadly-defined money stock (M3) during the three previous years, one can chart a clear parallel relationship. During the 1970s, the only breakdown of this relationship occurred in 1972; and, of course, that anomaly disappears when one adjusts the inflation data for the effects of the severe Phase II price controls in force in 1972.

In short, inflation is *not* caused by cost-pushes, wage-price spirals, depreciation of the dollar on foreign exchange markets, regulatory constraints, minimum wage laws, or lagging productivity growth. Inflation is a purely monetary phenomenon: when the purchasing power of the dollar falls steadily and persistently over many years, it is because dollars have steadily and persistently become more abundant in relation to the total quantity of real goods and services for which they exchange. Inflation, in sum, is caused by excessive growth of the money stock. Period.

The Government's Responsibility

As the Federal Reserve System authorities can control the rate of growth of the money stock, they clearly are to blame for its excessive expansion. Of course, the executive and legislative branches of the federal government have put heavy pressures on the monetary authorities to expand the money stock fast enough to "facilitate" the easy financing of the enormous, unprecedented peacetime deficits in the federal budget. In general, however, the Fed has been an easy touch, quite responsive to these pressures. William Miller, the current chairman of the Federal Reserve Board, has been variously described as "cooperative," a "team player," and "a tool of the [Carter] administration."[11] One wishes the central bankers had had more backbone.

If they had, we would have found that mere deficits, in the absence of excessive monetary expansion, can not cause inflation. Clearly, the deficits, working through the political process as it influences the Fed, *encourage* a loose monetary policy. But it is essential to recognize that it is the excessive growth of the money supply, whether to finance deficits or

for some other reason, that causes inflation. Conversely, with a sufficiently slow growth of the money stock, there can be no inflation, no
matter what is happening to the federal budget, labor costs, regulatory
standards, minimum wages, and so forth. To repeat, inflation is a purely
monetary phenomenon.

It hardly needs to be added that once excessive monetary expansion
has been halted, inflation cannot be kept alive merely by expectations of
inflation. People will find that, in the absence of continuing monetary
stimulation of aggregate expenditures, the inflation they expected just
doesn't happen. If they are obstinate and continue to act as if inflation is
not abating, they will simply price themselves out of their markets in the
same manner as the conspiring firm in the example above. It is far more
likely, however, that they will *adjust their expectations* as the rate of
inflation falls. Expectations cannot sustain an inflationary process unless
they are *validated* by the actual course of inflation; and that validation
can occur only so long as the growth of the money stock remains excessive.

---

1. Council of Economic Advisers, *Annual Report*, 1979, p. 84; emphasis added.
2. *Ibid.*, pp. 58-60.
3. *Ibid.*, p. 57.
4. *The Economic Report of the President*, 1979, p. 6.
5. Council of Economic Advisers, *Annual Report*, 1979, p. 55; emphasis added.
6. George Stigler and James K. Kindahl, "Industrial Prices, as Administered by Dr. Means," *American Economic Review*, 63 (Sept. 1973), p. 720.
7. Leonard W. Weiss, "The Role of Concentration in Recent Inflation," in Yale Brozen, ed., *The Competitive Economy: Selected Readings* (1975), pp. 206-212; and research by J. Fred Weston, cited in *Fortune* (March 26, 1979), p. 40.
8. George P. Shultz and Kenneth W. Dam, "The Life Cycle of Wage and Price Controls," in *Economic Policy Beyond the Headlines* (1977), p. 77.
9. Council of Economic Advisers, *Annual Report*, 1979, p. 239; latest price index values given are for November 1978.
10. Shultz and Dam, *op. cit.*, p. 78.
11. *The Wall Street Journal*, February 16, 1979.

Inflation: By-Product of Ideologies in Collision

by Wesley H. Hillendahl

The fact that man has endured ideological conflict since his beginning on earth is the central theme of the great scribes of all civilizations that have left records of their existence. While the predominant focus has been on moral philosophy, these ideological conflicts have ranged far and wide. They have pervaded the formal institutions of the church, government, commerce, finance, agriculture, and education as well as culture and the arts. In the present age the struggle centers on the law, the rules by which contemporary civilizations are ordered and under which individuals conduct their daily affairs with each other.

Whether man will be free to pursue his life and God-given destiny in an orderly environment in which government plays the domestic role of impartial umpire, or whether his life will be controlled in every detail by the dictums of an omnipotent materialistic bureaucracy is the central theme of today's conflict. Indeed, this is the essence of the catastrophic collision of economic thought of the nineteenth and twentieth centuries. Upon the outcome of this collision will depend man's way of life for generations to come. In simple economic terms, will the marketplace exist to serve the individual according to his choice, or will the market and the individual be under the control of the state?

Ideological Roots of the Free Market Economy

It is doubtful that a totally free market economy ever existed—one that is completely free of state intervention of one sort or another. And only in a few brief periods of recorded history has man been sufficiently motivated to assert himself to the degree required to grasp control of the market place from the hands of the rulers.[1] Such an event occurred in

Mr. Hillendahl, now retired, was Vice President and Director of Business Research of the Bank of Hawaii. This article, which appeared in the July 1974 issue of *The Freeman*, is reprinted by permission from his paper at a March 1974 seminar sponsored by The Committee for Monetary Research and Education.

1776 in America, but it was far from spontaneous. The spirit of '76 had been brewing for centuries in Europe. Its unique significance may be brought into focus by a brief review of several historical events. In this review, the essential distinction between the legal framework and the economic system must be kept in mind. It is all too easy to confuse the economic activities of a people with the legal framework under which they live, particularly today as government becomes increasingly involved in the economic affairs of its citizens.

The first of these historical incidents occurred on June 15, 1215 A. D. One recalls that King John of England was an oppressive tyrant. English noblemen and freemen became so incensed at the king's disregard for their rights that they pursued him to Runnymede where he was "convinced" to sign a document called the Magna Carta. This summit meeting produced a document which provided the concept of trial by jury, no taxation without representation, and the Writ of Habeas Corpus. It provided the fundamental restraint on government in the form of written law known throughout much of the world today.[2]

By 1628, the British King's disregard of individual rights won 400 years earlier became so insufferable that Parliament refused to vote any money to run the kingdom, and King Charles I was forced to sign the Petition of Right. This document provided the essential ingredients of personal security by restricting conditions relating to the levy of taxes, boarding of troops, declaration of martial law, trial by jury, and arbitrary imprisonment; without these rights, an individual cannot enjoy personal security.

In 1689, Parliament rebelled against King James II's tyrannical belief in absolute monarchy. Out of this action came the British Bill of Rights. Political liberty had triumphed in England, and with it a degree of economic freedom unknown before.

The profound significance to Americans of these early limitations on government is easily recognized, for in the first eight amendments to the Constitution of the United States, we find the influence of the Magna Carta, Petition of Right and the English Bill of Rights.

It was George Mason, the Virginian,[3] more than any other individual who forged the basic structure of limited and divided powers of government found in the United States Constitution and Bill of Rights. These are restrictive documents in the sense that they place more constraints on government than had ever prevailed in the past. The intent was to fragment political power, and to provide major obstacles to the reassembly of that power. In the wake of the centuries of tyranny, and the sacrifices of untold thousands of individuals in their struggle for freedom in England and Europe, the founders of the Republic were hardly likely to construct a government which could be centralized easily at the expense of individual liberty. The principle of separation or subdivision of powers, as championed by men such as Mason, is still history's most effective stumbling block for tyrants. However, the Constitution was not perfect, and it was George Mason who foresaw the fatal flaws introduced by compromise that ultimately became the avenues by which much of it has been struck down.

In 1850, a French statesman, economist and author, Frederic Bastiat, espoused the theme of limited government at a time when France was turning to socialism or total bureaucracy, following the French Revolution in 1848—which had coincided with the release of Marx's Manifesto. Bastiat emphasized the essential spiritual antecedents in the framework of economic freedom. He commenced his book *The Law* with the following: "We hold from God the gift which includes all others. This gift is life—physical, intellectual, and moral life. . . . Life, liberty, and property do not exist because men have made laws. On the contrary, it was the fact that life, liberty, and property existed beforehand that caused men to make laws in the first place."[4]

It is all but forgotten by many today that the State is not the source of liberty and property; these are inalienable rights that come from God.

Bastiat expressed the issue clearly: "What, then, is law? It is the collective organization of the individual right to lawful defense. Each of us has a natural right—from God—to defend his person, his liberty, and his property; and by extension it follows that a group of men have the right to organize and support a common force to protect these rights constantly."

He concluded, ". . . since an individual cannot lawfully use force against the person, liberty or property of another individual, then the common force—for the same reason—cannot lawfully be used to destroy the person, liberty, or property of individuals or groups." In Bastiat's eyes, any form of state intervention in the affairs of the individual is not only illegal, it is immoral and contrary to God's law.

Thus did Bastiat so eloquently summarize what had evolved over hundreds of years—the legal framework of the constraints on government that make it possible for each of us to order his own life, and to offer his service in the manner called "free enterprise."

Here then are the moral and spiritual antecedents of the American system as codified in the law forming the framework of the free market economy. Being all but forgotten today under the pressure of the conflict, these principles are restated here because they constitute the *raison d'être* for any meaningful monetary and economic reform.

Accomplishments of the Free Market

Having established a Republic under the legal framework of limited government, what could man accomplish in the free market?

In the beginning the focus was mainly on the family, the community, and the job of survival. By 1840, 70 percent of the people in the United States still lived on farms, while more than 90 percent grew their own food. Not satisfied with devoting most of his energies to the drudgery of survival, the free individual American, possessed of a drive to better himself, undertook an unprecedented change in his way of life.

The age-old concept that man's material wealth is limited, which had arisen out of the fact that human energy had never been effectively augmented, gave way to the principle that material wealth could be expanded to an almost unlimited extent by multiplying limited natural resources and limited human energy by tools using nonhuman energy.

During the 1800s, a massive reconstruction of the application of labor was brought about through the invention of a host of machines which permitted the augmentation of human effort by non-human energy. Initially, wood and whale oil were the principal sources of energy. These gave way in time to petroleum products, the use of which doubled decade after decade until early in the twentieth century.

In agriculture, the first significant invention, the steel-bladed plow, occurred in 1841. In rapid succession came the power reaper, the steam thrasher, and the haying machine. Then in 1884, the first combine and the first tractor appeared. All of the things we take for granted today were marvelous inventions in those days. Can you visualize yourself pitching hay or performing some other type of hand labor on a farm before being rescued by these marvelous machines?

After the turn of the century, a whole succession of specialized tools and machines were developed which bring food all the way from the farm to the home refrigerator. As a consequence of these labor-saving inventions, the 70 percent of people on farms in 1840 had been reduced by one-half by the turn of the century. Continuing advancement to World War II brought the proportion of people on farms to 18 percent. Today, only about 5 percent of the population live on farms, and farm labor accounts for only 4 percent of the nation's labor force. At no time in history nor in any other country has there been such extensive productive application of man's inventive genius—and the process seems endless.

Economic freedom has, by similar processes, provided an enormous expansion of physical and mental productivity, and offered the incentive to develop the vast array of items that have become the underpinning of our standard of living. We've had the incentive to solve disease and sanitation problems, provide housing for the entire population, develop great centers for preserving and transmitting our accumulated learning, and transfer goods via a vast production, distribution, and marketing mechanism unknown in history.

The Roots of the Controlled Economy

At the heart of the notion that the economy must be controlled by the government are several well recognized themes: (1) the concept that society is made up of two classes, the oppressed and the oppressors, the "class struggle," (2) the concept of "exploitation" of man by man, and (3) the concept that the controlled order is inevitable as the consequence of the inexorable increase in impoverishment caused by the development of capitalism.

Hence, by revolution as advocated by some, such as the secret League of Just Men who had commissioned Marx to write their *Manifesto*, or by evolution as advocated by the British Fabian Society or the Americans for Democratic Action, "... It is necessary to emancipate society at large from exploitation, oppression, class distinctions, and class struggles."

The economic and political measures by which collectivists intend to convert society generally include:[6]

1. Abolition of private property and the rental thereof to individuals by the state.
2. A heavily progressive income tax.
3. Abolition of all right of inheritance.

4. Government control of credit by means of a monopolistic central bank.

5. Government control of communications, transportation, and means of production.

6. Abolition of distinctions between urban and rural areas by redistribution of population.

7. Free government schooling.

These features of the welfare state, socialism, the planned economy—call it what you will—are recited, not as we recited the roots of the free market which are all but forgotten, but because they are so conspicuous in today's economy that we are inclined to overlook what they really are—the legal framework for the very antithesis of the free market which this country's founding fathers envisioned.

Ideologies in Collision

Both Marx and Bastiat expressed concern for the common man under the tyranny which had prevailed for centuries in Europe and England. But Marx advocated as a substitute for the monarchy a new form of tyranny—a bureaucracy supported by a synthetic majority rule; whereas Bastiat and his English counterparts correctly envisioned that only by placing all forms of tyranny in the chains of restrictive law could man arise out of repression.

Hence, the industrial revolution in America, operating under the aegis of a Constitutional Republic providing maximum freedom for the individual and a minimum of exploitation, bore fruit as nowhere else in the world. Instead of the exploitation and oppression, anticipated by Marx, has come the emancipation of the masses seen in the visions of the founding fathers.

However, while vast economic changes were occurring throughout the Western world and in America in particular over the last century, government was also undergoing a transformation of major proportions. From an inconsequential power over economic affairs during the nineteenth century, the federal government today has become the most powerful bureaucracy on earth, and has regressed into a massive engine for control and redistribution of people and wealth, largely as Marx and his colleagues had advocated.

Much of what government has undertaken domestically falls within the prescribed limits of the role of referee. However, the main thrust of government activity in recent years has gone far beyond the prescribed limits. F. A. Hayek, in *The Constitution of Liberty*,[7] foretold the consequences of practices which have developed under persistent pressure to do away with those limitations on government which were erected for the protection of individual liberty.

"This conflict between the ideal of freedom and the desire to 'correct' the distribution of incomes so as to make it more 'just' is usually not clearly recognized. . . .

But the ultimate result . . . will necessarily be, not a modification of the existing order, but its complete abandonment and its replacement by an altogether different system—the command economy."

Hayek is one of the few writers who correctly recognized the mixed economy for what it is—an unstable transitional condition between the free market economy and the bureaucratically controlled society.

Inflation in the Transitional Period

While those who champion the sanctity of individual liberty and the ideal of the free market deplore the transition, socialist scholars are inclined to want to get on with the work of erecting the bureaucracy and eradicating all vestiges of their bogy man, "laissez-faire" enterprise. Be that as it may, it is the contemporary status of this transition that invites our closer examination. Specifically, our concern is the phenomenon of inflation in the mixed economy as a manifestation of the transition.

Because many qualified economists have demonstrated the essential monetary nature of inflation, we need not restate here the distinction between money and credit expansion and the resultant rise in wages and prices, nor go into the fine points of monetizing debt.

There is a prevailing notion that in the transition period during which functions performed by the private sector of the economy are transferred to government, inflation will persist as long as the still-strong private sector and the growing public sector fight for the limited amount of capital.

However, many economists seem only recently to be grasping the fact that as the transition progresses, so must monetary inflation proceed at an accelerated rate. The long standing argument that the manner in which government debt is funded is a determining factor in inflation, seems inadequate to explain the evident fact that inflation is accelerating.

The problem is that too much attention has been devoted to national income analysis while ignoring the nation's balance sheet. An examination of practically all measures of balance sheet liquidity or cash reserves reveals that the private sector of the economy is being progressively starved of funds by rising taxes and increasing costs of nonproductive overhead caused by governmental interventions.

Expanding Government

Empirically, the record in the United States shows that so long as all governments combined took in direct and indirect taxes less than 25 percent of personal income, some discretion existed as to what rate of monetary inflation could be undertaken at any given time. However, once government expanded beyond the range, as it did years ago, the economy embarked on a one-way street; and as government grows progressively larger at the expense of the private sector, so must inflation proceed apace to accommodate the credit requirements of the economy.[8]

Because government spending has expanded to more than 43 percent of personal income, this progressive expansion of credit is necessary to avoid collapse as the level of borrowing must also accelerate in lieu of diminishing residual profits and retained earnings.

Ultimately, as government proceeds progressively to confiscate all earnings, one might expect monetary inflation to reach proportions experienced in France in the 1790s, Germany in the 1920s, Russia immediately after the so-called revolution, and Hungary in 1946.

However, before hyperinflation of such proportions would be generated, it is more likely that an attempt toward the conversion to a totally controlled economy will be undertaken under the guise of some combination of "emergencies." Many of the mechanisms to achieve such a conversion have been on the books for many years.[9] And Congress delegates additional "emergency powers" to the bureaucracy as each new "crisis" is engineered.

Meanwhile, unforeseen developments such as the projection of the Middle East conflict into the otherwise inevitable domestic oil shortage may produce profound and undefinable effects on the future timing and nature of the conversion, not only in the United States, but worldwide. It is clear that the Arab nations have administered the *coup de grace* to the faltering International Monetary Fund, and that the role of gold is about to achieve a significance in world monetary affairs virtually inconceivable in the United States only a few years ago.

Inflation in the Controlled Economy

It is not our purpose here to enter into a theoretical discussion of inflation under socialism, but rather to suggest two thoughts. First, utopian goals of inflation-free prosperity for all, as envisioned by the planners of the multinational political economy, may be quite unrealistic.

The end product of the transition from the free market to socialism even in America may well produce vastly different results than expected. Simply stated, a bureaucratically controlled economy is incapable of maintaining a level of production adequate to sustain itself. In the absence of the profit motive, people will not produce at their capacity, and in the absence of a mechanism to retain and utilize savings, the machinery of production will either run down or wear out. Even more significant is the underlying moral issue. Let us heed Garet Garrett's words :[10]

> When in the conquest of power and for political ends a government deliberately engineers inflation . . . the people will lose control of [government] . . . and finally, the revelry of public money, which for a while seems to cost nobody anything, brings to pass a state of moral obliquity throughout society. The monetary debacle is relatively unimportant. The moral debacle is cancerous and possibly incurable.

Who, then, under the controlled economy will have the incentive to continue to produce the economic abundance from which has been drawn the hundreds of billions of dollars of foreign aid designed to prop up untold socialist experiments in a hundred or more countries, the numerous unsupportable and uneconomic public infrastructures,[11] the vast nonproductive, self-defeating bureaucracies set up in many so-called developing nations to divide the free loot?

Can Russia Survive?

But of even greater significance, what will be the fate of the USSR, the greatest socialist experiment of all time? This question may sound strange in the context that the USSR is presented to us as an economy based on such a highly advanced technology that it poses a vast military threat to which we must respond by spending over $80 billion annually on armaments.

Under the Czar, Russia was well advanced into the industrial revolution, and at the turn of the century, was the world's leading oil exporter. But such pre-revolutionary developments are portrayed as insignificant in terms of the Soviet's achievements of the past 50 years.

However, the record shows that present day Soviet technology is synthetic—it has all been imported. Based on ten years of research into official documents, Antony C. Sutton, research fellow at the Hoover Institution on War, Revolution and Peace, developed grounds for his widely quoted testimony before the Republican Party National Convention in 1972.

In Sutton's words: "There is no such thing as Soviet technology. Almost all—perhaps 90-95 percent—came directly or indirectly from the United States and its allies. In effect, the United States and the NATO countries have built the Soviet Union. Its industrial *and* its military capabilities. This massive construction job has taken 50 years, since the revolution in 1917. It has been carried out through trade and the sale of plants, equipment and technical assistance."[12]

Sutton also quoted Ambassador Harriman: "Stalin paid tribute to the assistance rendered by the United States to Soviet industry before and during the War. Stalin said that about two-thirds of all large industrial enterprises in the Soviet Union has been built with the United States' help or technical assistance."

The West Helps Russia

In his three-volume work, *Western Technology and Soviet Economic Development*[13] covering 1917 to 1965, Sutton demonstrates on an industry-by-industry basis that the West has contributed under contract essentially all the plants and technology which comprise the Soviet military-industrial complex today.

Of great significance is his statement that it has been shown Russia has never suffered from a dearth of competent technical and scientific personnel, rather the bureaucracy is incapable of translating the endeavors of individuals into productive results.

The power of his statement is that it is not theoretical, but is based on the observed record. Its significance lies in the application of Garrett's observation regarding the cancerous moral debacle which occurs under bureaucratic control. In basic English: People cannot be forced to produce effectively without personal incentives to do so. And socialism demonstrably fails to provide these essential incentives.

In my opinion, the death of the free market in the United States would come not as a sudden depression, but rather a gradual sinking into stagnation in activity characteristic of controlled economies. The drying up of that enormous production by which much of the so-called free world is subsidized would also cause the stagnation to extend abroad. Finally, the stream of technology upon which the Iron Curtain countries have relied for 50 years would dry up, and the Soviets, for the first time in their existence, would be cast free to sink or swim on their own.

Socialism Precludes Inflation?

The second thought I wish to examine more carefully is the notion that inflation is a product of sound monetary practices, irrespective of the type of economy or political framework. Let us not forget that one of Napoleon's first acts was to restore the gold standard in France.

As to the alleged freedom from inflation in a world under socialism, we may turn to economist Benjamin Anderson :[14]

By 1921, Lenin had reached the conclusion that pure communism would not work, and the New Economic Policy announced by Lenin in 1921, frankly acknowledged a partial return to capitalism. The reestablishment of capitalism in Russia involved the redevelopment of a money held as closely as possible at a parity with gold. In the years that followed, Russia had repeated slumps in the value of its currency, but always resisted them, and finally turned decisively toward heavy gold production, recognizing the need of gold both for international use and as an element of strength in the domestic currency situation....Russia could never make its paper money a "thing in itself" created by the state and held fixed by the state's fiat.

Currently, the Soviet Union holds gold in such high esteem that the first of four nuclear power plants was recently activated to power gold dredges and other mining machinery at the Soviets' principal gold mining center of Bilibino in Siberia.

Hence, it would appear that in the totally socialized world, civilization would descend into stagnation for an untold period of time. If such economy as remains in the world is to be free of inflation, it could be accomplished only by recourse to that perennial barbarian, gold.

The Solution—A Moral Issue

Although we are far down the road, this dismal outcome of the ideological collision need not occur—indeed, we must not permit it to occur. However, mere monetary constraint will no longer provide an effective answer because of the balance sheet liquidity problem. Restoration of a sound gold convertible currency is a move in the right direction; but if Anderson's observations regarding the Soviet Union are valid, such a move will not, in itself, eradicate the bureaucracy. Only by attacking the ideological roots of socialism can the tide be turned in practice. This means checking the growth of government and the spawn of monopoly industries which through the centuries have always fed on centralized power. This means returning government to its constitutionally authorized role and restoring true competition to the marketplace.

In the final analysis, the issue is a moral one: Are enough people willing to exercise sufficient individual initiative, responsibility and integrity to do the job?

In the abstract, this seems to be a reasonable challenge. But in practice, how many businessmen who espouse free enterprise for their own businesses will give up the practice of using their influence with their legislators to limit competition or otherwise gain economic advantage through the legislative process?

How many businessmen will sacrifice profits in a genuine compassion for their fellow man by giving up their lucrative business with the bureaucrats of countries who have sent millions of their citizens to their death in slave labor camps?

How many businessmen will voluntarily undertake the necessary expenditures to control their factory effluents in the interest of cleaning up genuine environmental health hazards, or will do the same for their employees by minimizing work hazards?

How many labor union leaders will acknowledge that they can obtain more jobs and better working conditions for the rank and file union members by allowing companies to make higher profits for capital formation rather than by extracting maximum wage and fringe benefits at the bargaining table?

How many able-bodied people who are racketeering on welfare will voluntarily go back to work?

How many legislators will stand in the face of the pressures of those bent on selfish gains and stop the legal plunder? And of equal importance, how many legislators will stand for election on constitutional principles instead of offering even more legal plunder?

How many government bureaucrats will voluntarily husband public funds, trim dead wood from their departments, and phase out unnecessary operations? These are examples of individual human actions. Ludwig von Mises, who was acknowledged to be the greatest contemporary champion of the free market, has shown that economics is the aggregate of individual human action. Whether a society is basically moral or immoral in total depends on the degree of morality of the actions of each individual in it. Inflation is the aggregate result of legal plunder—as such, it represents the epitome of immorality.

In a totalitarian society, the problem of inflation, like any other, can be controlled at any time by government decree, but only at an unmeasurable cost in loss of personal liberty. In a free society, control over inflation can be accomplished only when its underlying causes are held in check by the predominance of individuals motivated by moral principles and acting with economic responsibility.

Only when sufficient people recognize the moral nature of the problem and are willing to act accordingly will the surge toward the command economy be reversed.

---

1. Henry Grady Weaver, *The Mainspring of Human Progress* (Irvington-on-Hudson, N. Y.: The Foundation for Economic Education, 1993).

2. James Mussatti, *The Constitution of the United States* (Princeton, N. J.: D. Van Nostrand Company, Inc., 1960).

3. George Mason, *Architect of Constitutional Liberty* (Fullerton, Calif.: Education Information, Inc.).

4. Frederic Bastiat, *The Law*, (Irvington-on-Hudson, N. Y.: The Foundation for Economic Education, 1993).

5. Warren T. Hackett, *How We Prosper Under Freedom* (Washington, D. C.: Citizens Evaluation Institute).

6. Karl Marx, *Communist Manifesto* (Chicago: Henry Regnery Company, 1965).

7. F. A. Hayek, *The Constitution of Liberty* (Chicago: University of Chicago Press, 1960).

8. Wesley H. Hillendahl, *Big Government's Destruction of the American Economy* (Honolulu: Bank of Hawaii, April, 1973).

9. Executive Order 11490, Assigning Preparedness Functions to Federal Departments and Agencies, *Federal Register*, Volume 34, No. 209, Part II, October 30, 1969.

10. Garet Garrett, *The People's Pottage* (Caldwell, Idaho: The Caxton Printers, Inc., 1965).

11. All too frequently American taxpayers' dollars have been used to provide infrastructures which to date have done little to improve the status of the average citizen of developing nations; instead, the benefits have accrued largely to the profits of multinational corporations which have located plants in these low-cost labor markets.

12. Antony C. Sutton, *National Suicide, Military Aid to the Soviet Union* (New Rochelle, N. Y.: Arlington House, 1973).

13. Antony C. Sutton, *Western Technology and Soviet Economic Development, 1917...1965* (Stanford, Calif.: Hoover Institution of War, Revolution and Peace, Stanford University, 1968).

14. Benjamin M. Anderson, *Economics and the Public Welfare* (Princeton, N. J.: D. Van Nostrand Company, Inc., 1949).

Edmund Burke on Inflation and Despotism

by Gary North

Edmund Burke is generally regarded as one of the founders of modern conservative thought. As a defender of tradition, private property, slow social change, and "muddling through," he was an opponent of aprioristic thinking, rationalistic blueprints for social reconstruction, and "metaphysical arithmeticians." He is therefore not heralded as a master of the subtle skills of economic reasoning. Nevertheless, Burke's teachings on the relationship between policies of monetary debasement and social change indicate that he was far more alert to the dangers of monetary inflation than are recent defenders of Federal deficits and a system of price-wage controls. When *Nation's Business* can survey 450 leading business executives concerning their opinions on price and wage controls, and find that over 70 percent of them favor the controls, with 47 percent of them favoring an indefinite extension of such controls, it is not difficult to conclude that Edmund Burke had a more sophisticated sense of economics than our modern professionals.[1]

In 1790, Burke distinguished himself by writing what was to become the classic statement of conservative social theory, *Reflections on the Revolution in France.* Though its focus is social and political, the book contains several penetrating sections dealing with two crucial economic issues: wealth redistribution and monetary debasement. His presuppositions are not those of classical liberalism, given his commitment to landed property as distinguished from commercial ("monied") property, but his conclusions are quite close to nineteenth-century liberal monetary theories.

Burke's defense of private property in land as a form of ownership superior to stocks, bonds, and other "paper" investments harkens back to the famous Putney Debates of Cromwell's Army in 1647. Burke, like Ireton (Cromwell's son-in-law) before him, viewed the owners of landed property as men with a greater stake in the preservation of society than

---

Dr. North is President of the Institute for Christian Economics, Tyler, Texas. This article is reprinted from the February 1973 issue of *The Freeman.*

either the propertyless or those owning nonlanded property.[2] Understandably, given this perspective, Burke was appalled by the advent of money speculators in France, coupled with the simultaneous confiscation of church and Crown lands. "The monied interest is in its nature more ready for any adventure," he wrote, "and its possessors more disposed to new enterprises of any kind. Being of a recent acquisition, it falls in more naturally with any novelties. It is therefore the kind of wealth which will be resorted to by all who wish for change."[3] Burke was not opposed to change as such; he wrote that any state "without the means of some change is without the means of its conservation."[4] But he wanted slow, steady, familiar, "organic changes, and not the more rapid changes associated with modern industrial society. In this sense, he was certainly a "conservative" rather than a "liberal."

This preference for landed property—which in eighteenth-century England meant property hedged about by statist restrictions on ownership, transfer of such ownership, inheritance, and politically imposed land enclosures[5]—over monied property undoubtedly colored Burke's economic analysis. He resented what he regarded as land confiscation in France and the sale of this land to middle-class French businessmen, thereby "carrying on a process of continual transmutation of paper into land, and land into paper. . . . By this means the spirit of money-jobbing and speculation goes into the mass of land itself and incorporates with it."[6] Yet he accepted Parliamentary enclosure bills, and he was personally interested in agricultural rationalization and improvement for England's increasingly market-oriented system of farming. Indeed, as Professor Herbert Heaton has written, "Burke discussed cabbages and pigs almost as earnestly as he did the grievances of the American colonies."[7] Thus, he was not fully consistent in his support of private ownership nor in his attacks on political confiscation.

Immorality and Instability

His real concern was with morality and with semifeudal concepts like honor and loyalty. These concepts were being undermined in France by revolutionary politics and monetary debasement on the part of the French government. Instability — Burke's greatest fear — was becoming the order of the day in France. Most serious, this instability was undermining the French family, that most fundamental of all institutions in conservative social analysis.

> Nothing stable in the modes of holding property or exercising function could form a solid ground on which any parent could speculate in the education of his offspring or in a choice for their future establishment in the world. No principles would be early worked into the habits....Who would insure a tender and delicate sense of honor to beat almost with the first pulses of the heart when no man could know what would be the test of honor in a nation continually varying the standard of its coin?[8]

The result of such an unsettled commonwealth, Burke predicted, would be barbarism. What was to take place in France over the decade following the publication of the *Reflections* convinced many of his contemporaries of the accuracy of his prediction.

France, it should not be forgotten, was probably the wealthiest nation on earth in the final quarter of the eighteenth century, although the English were rapidly overtaking their French neighbors, and by 1800 had probably succeeded in becoming the world's richest citizens. Burke understood the position of the French better than the French revolutionaries did; he praised France's cities, the transportation system, French agriculture, manufacturing, charitable foundations, and scholars.[9] But the French state was also in debt — so heavily in debt that half of all the King's revenues went in interest payments on the debt. (England was in a similar situation, and Burke may have been hinting at this fact in the *Reflections*.[10])

> Nations are wading deeper and deeper into an ocean of boundless debt. Public debts, which at first were a security to governments by interesting many in the public tranquility [a variation of an argument used by Alexander Hamilton in 1790 in his Report on Public Credit[11]] are likely in their excess to become the means of their subversion. If governments provide for these debts by heavy impositions, they perish by becoming odious to the people.[12]

Burke, like Hamilton, failed to see that a "little" governmental indebtedness is comparable to a little unwanted pregnancy, but he did grasp the politically unsettling reality of heavy state debt. Such conditions lead to revolution. (The French Estates General were summoned in order to approve tax increases necessary to finance the French debt; this was the first great event in the French Revolution.) Burke feared this repercussion of state debt because, he said, revolutions "are favorable to confiscation; and it is impossible to know under what obnoxious names the next confiscations will be authorized."[13]

Monetization of Debt

Like so many politicians before and since, the French revolutionaries decided that the best possible way of getting out of debt was to go deeper into debt. The Anglo-American version of this system is through the monetization of debt, through the mechanism of a central bank and fractional reserve commercial banks.[14] The French leaders adopted a somewhat different system. They first confiscated the lands of the church and Crown. Then they issued paper debt certificates, called *assignats,* that could be used in the purchase of these lands. These certificates bore 5 percent interest at first, lowered to 3 percent a few months after the initial offering in 1789. The decree of April 17, 1790, made these legal tender. These were "given" to—forced upon—those holding other forms of state debt certificates.[15] In the words of Professor Bosher, who is not hostile to these administrative reforms, "Any of the alternative methods put forward would have perpetuated the old private enterprise system."[16]

The value of these fiat notes fell almost immediately. The "temporary" expedient of inflation and legal tender laws became a permanent phenomenon. The 400 million of them issued in 1789 became a roaring flood of 40 billion within four years. Again, quoting Bosher: "A decree of 8 April 1793 ordered all government purchases and payments to soldiers to be in *assignats.* Three days later, the Convention prohibited circulation, sale or purchase of gold and silver coin. All transactions were henceforth to be in *assignats,* now the principal legal currency."[17] The penalty (not mentioned by Bosher): imprisonment for six years.[18] Andrew Dickson White's *Fiat Money Inflation in France* continues the analysis:

> Later, on September 8, 1793, the penalty for such offenses was made death, with confiscation of the criminal's property, and a

reward was offered to any person informing the authorities regarding any such criminal transaction. To reach the climax of ferocity, the Convention decreed, in May 1794, that the death penalty should be inflicted on any person convicted of "having asked, before a bargain was concluded, in what money payment was to be made."[19]

It is not surprising that an increase of circulation from 400 million to 40 billion in a span of four years would have produced price inflation. What is surprising is that a book seriously advertising itself as "conservative economics" could argue, as one widely read study does, that, "The fact that they were destroyed as money by the gigantic counterfeiting operations of the money creators later, does not detract from their validity."[20] Burke, almost two centuries ago, knew better than that!

Price and Wage Controls

On September 29, 1793, the "Law of the Maximum" was declared, setting forth a system of price and wage controls. But, as White says, it "could not be made to work well—even by the shrewdest devices. In the greater part of France it could not be enforced."[21] It was abolished in the latter months of 1794, a total disaster. It was as unworkable as the early attempts to control prices and wages had been in New England, and it was as disastrous as the controls had been in the American Revolution.[22]

Burke had foreseen these events in 1790. The politics of mass inflation, he warned, would create a gambler mentality in the minds of French citizens, a mad rush to stay ahead of rising prices. He warned the citizens of France—or at least those who might be reading his book—of this fact:

> Your legislators, in everything new, are the very first who have founded a commonwealth on gaming, and infused this spirit into it as its vital breath. The great object of these politics is to metamorphose France from a great kingdom into one great playtable; to turn its inhabitants into a nation of gamesters; . . . With you a man can neither earn nor buy his dinner without a speculation. What he receives in the morning will not have the same value at night. . . . Industry must wither away. Economy must be driven from your country. Careful provision will have no existence.[23]

It is not simply that industry will decline or that people will have to become speculators. The real curse of mass inflation is that it harms the ignorant, the unprotected, the citizen who is not aware of the nature of the new, inflationary game. In the name of democracy, the French revolutionaries had constructed a system that favors the elite—an elite made up of the least honorable, least productive men in the community.

> The truly melancholy part of the policy of systematically making a nation of gamesters is this, that though all are forced to play, few can understand the game; and fewer still are in a condition to avail themselves of the knowledge. The many must be the dupes of the few who conduct the machine of these speculations. What effect it must have on the country people is visible. The townsmen can calculate from day to day, not so the inhabitant of the country. When the peasant first brings his corn to market, the magistrate in the towns obliges him to take the *assignat* at par; when he goes to the shop with the money, he finds it seven percent worse for crossing the way. This market he will not readily resort to again. The townspeople will be inflamed; they will force the country people to bring their corn.[24]

The nation will be torn with social conflict. This, in turn, will create disruptions, further instability, and the destruction of law and order. His warnings were in vain, and his prophecies came true.

Convertibility Makes a Difference

There is a difference, he said, between the paper money of England and that of France, contrary to certain French writers. "They forget that, in England, not one shilling of paper money of any description is received but of choice; and that it is convertible at pleasure, in an instant and without the smallest loss, into cash [specie] again."[25] The Napoleonic Wars were to bring an end to convertibility in England for temporary periods, but Burke's polemical point was grounded in fact: the presence of the threat of specie demands by the public acted as a restraint on the process of fractional reserve banking, thus reducing the extent of monetary inflation. But French leaders have gone mad, he said:

The only difference among their financial factions is on the greater or the lesser quantity of *assignats* to be imposed on the public sufferance. They are all professors of *assignats*. Even those whose natural good sense and knowledge of commerce, not obliterated by philosophy [by which Burke meant the *a priori* theories of Enlightenment theorists], furnish decisive arguments against this delusion conclude their arguments by proposing the emission of *assignats*. I suppose they must talk of *assignats,* as no other language would be understood. All experience of their inefficiency does not in the least discourage them. Are the old *assignats* depreciated at market? What is the remedy? Issue new *assignats*.[26]

Burke's jibes at the self-deceived and self-assured manipulators could (and perhaps someday will) be lodged against our contemporary "metaphysical arithmeticians," the inflation-minded econometricians:

In all this procedure I can see neither the solid sense of plain dealing nor the subtle dexterity of ingenious fraud. The objections within the Assembly to pulling up the floodgates for this inundation of fraud are unanswered, but they are thoroughly refuted by a hundred thousand financiers in the street. These are the numbers by which the metaphysic arithmeticians compute. These are the grand calculations on which a philosophical public credit is founded in France. They cannot raise supplies, but they can raise mobs.[27]

The people of France ought to see where a philosophy of state theft is leading them:

I see the confiscators begin with bishops and chapters, and monasteries, but I do not see them end there....Flushed with the insolence of their first inglorious victories, and pressed by the distresses caused by their lust of unhallowed lucre, disappointed but not discouraged, they have at length ventured completely to subvert all property of all descriptions throughout the extent of a great kingdom. They have compelled all men, in all transactions of commerce, in the disposal of lands, in civil dealing, and through the whole communion of life, to accept as perfect payment and good and lawful tender the symbols of their speculations on a projected sale of their plunder. What vestiges of liberty or property have they left?[28]

Once begun, this madness will be compounded. "If possible, the next Assembly must be worse than the present. The present, by destroying and altering everything, will leave to their successors apparently nothing popular to do. They will be roused by emulation and example to enterprises the boldest and the most absurd."[29] This, of course, is precisely what was to take place in France. "So violent an outrage upon credit, property, and liberty as this compulsory paper currency has seldom been exhibited by the alliance of bankruptcy and tyranny, at any time or in any nation."[30] Yet it got much worse in the next five years.

Theft is an insidious philosophy, whether public or private in scope. Short-run benefits of the confiscation of another's property tempt men to expand their activities and bring on personal and national disaster. Burke's warnings went unheeded by the French government in 1790. Today's metaphysical arithmeticians consider such opinions as Burke's utterly narrow, dogmatic, and unenlightened by the principles of modern thought. The results of today's confiscators will be comparable to the results of the French Revolution, since the principles are similar. If not mass inflation, then it will be some Napoleon of the mass media. Perhaps it may be both.

---

1. *Nation's Business* (July, 1972), pp. 28 ff.

2. See Ireton's remarks in A. S. P. Woodhouse (ed.), *Puritanism and Liberty* (London: Dent., 1938), pp. 52ff., 64ff. On the setting of the Putney Debates, see Robert S. Paul, *The Lord Protector: Religion and Politics in the Life of Oliver Cromwell* (Grand Rapids: Eerdmans, 1955), Chap. 7.

3. Burke, *Reflections on the Revolution in France,* edited by Thomas H. D. Mahoney (Indianapolis: Bobbs-Merrill, Liberal Arts Press, 1955), p. 126.

4. *Ibid.,* p. 24.

5. Cf. Christopher Hill, *Reformation to Industrial Revolution* (Baltimore: Penguin, 1969), p. 270; Herbert Heaton, *Economic History of Europe* (rev. ed., New York: Harper & Row, 1948), pp. 413-14, 419; Shepard B. Clough, *The Economic Development of Western Civilization* (New York: McGraw-Hill, 1959), pp. 296-97.

6. *Reflections,* p. 224.

7. Heaton, p. 410.

8. *Reflections,* p. 108.

9. *Ibid.,* p. 151.

10. J. F. Bosher, *French Finances, 1770- 1795* (New York: Cambridge University Press, 1970), p. 24.

11. Hamilton wrote in his First Report on Public Credit (1790): "If all the public creditors

receive their dues from one source, distributed with an equal hand, their interest will be the same. And, having the same interests, they will unite in the support of the fiscal arrangements of the Government...." Robert Birley (ed.), *Speeches and Documents in American History* (New York: Oxford University Press, 1951), Vol. 1, p. 159. Yet, as Prof. John C. Miller notes, "The national debt, instead of cementing the nation politically, acted as a *divisive* force. . . ." *Alexander Hamilton and the Growth of the New Nation* (New York: Harper Torchbook, 1964), p. 255.

12. *Reflections*, pp. 178-79.

13. *Ibid.*

14. Charles Holt Carroll, writing for *Hunt's Merchants' Magazine* in the 1850s and 1860s, produced some excellent analyses of the process of the monetization of debt: *Organization of Debt into Currency and Other Papers* (New York: Arno Press, 1971). This was the essence of Hamilton's "sinking fund": Miller, p. 257. It is also the essence of the Open Market Committee of the Federal Reserve System: Herbert V. Prochnow (ed.), *The Federal Reserve System* (New York: Harper & Bros., 1961), Chap. 7.

15. Bosher, pp. 273-74.

16. *Ibid.*, p. 273.

17. *Ibid.*, p. 274.

18. Andrew Dickson White, *Fiat Money Inflation in France* (Foundation for Economic Education, [1912] 1959), pp. 78-79.

19. *Ibid.*, p. 79.

20. Gertrude Coogan, *Money Creators* (Hawthorne, Calif.: Omni Books, [1935] 1963), p. 320. For a critical analysis of the writings of Miss Coogan, see my essay, "Gertrude Coogan and the Myth of Social Credit," *An Introduction to Christian Economics* (Nutley, N. J.: Craig Press, 1973).

21. White, p. 77.

22. On Puritan economic controls, see Richard B. Morris, *Government and Labor in Early America* (New York: Columbia University Press, 1946), pp. 56 ff. These tended to die out after 1675. On the controls during the American Revolution, see Percy Greaves, "From Price Control to Valley Forge," *The Freeman* (February, 1972).

23. *Reflections,* pp. 226-27.

24. *Ibid.*, p. 227.

25. *Ibid.*, p. 273. When Burke speaks of "cash" he means "specie": p. 283.

26. *Ibid.*, p. 276.

27. *Ibid.*, p. 281.

28. *Ibid.*, pp. 174-75.

29. *Ibid.*, p. 232.

30. *Ibid.*, p. 141.

II. SAPPING THE FOUNDATION

Inflation

by Ludwig von Mises

If the supply of caviar were as plentiful as the supply of potatoes, the price of caviar—that is, the exchange ratio between caviar and money or caviar and other commodities—would change considerably. In that case, one could obtain caviar at a much smaller sacrifice than is required today. Likewise, if the quantity of money is increased, the purchasing power of the monetary unit decreases, and the quantity of goods that can be obtained for one unit of this money decreases also.

When, in the sixteenth century, American resources of gold and silver were discovered and exploited, enormous quantities of the precious metals were transported to Europe. The result of this increase in the quantity of money was a general tendency toward an upward movement of prices. In the same way, today, when a government increases the quantity of paper money, the result is that the purchasing power of the monetary unit begins to drop, and so prices rise. This is called *inflation.*

Unfortunately, in the United States, as well as in other countries, some people prefer to attribute the cause of inflation not to an increase in the quantity of money but, rather, to the rise in prices.

However, there has never been any serious argument against the economic interpretation of the relationship between prices and the quantity of money, or the exchange ratio between money and other goods, commodities, and services. Under present-day technological conditions there is nothing easier than to manufacture pieces of paper upon which certain monetary amounts are printed. In the United States, where all the notes are of the same size, it does not cost the government more to print a bill of a thousand dollars than it does to print a bill of one dollar. It is purely a printing procedure that requires the same quantity of paper and ink.

In the eighteenth century, when the first attempts were made to issue

Ludwig von Mises (1881-1973) was one of the great defenders of a rational economic science, and perhaps the single most creative mind at work in this field in our country. This article, adapted from a lecture delivered in Argentina in late 1959, was printed in The *Freeman,* March 1980. It appears as a chapter in *Economic Policy: Thoughts for Today and Tomorrow.*

bank notes and to give these bank notes the quality of legal tender—that is, the right to be honored in exchange transactions in the same way that gold and silver pieces were honored—the governments and nations believed that bankers had some secret knowledge enabling them to produce wealth out of nothing. When the governments of the eighteenth century were in financial difficulties, they thought all they needed was a clever banker at the head of their financial management in order to get rid of all their difficulties.

Some years before the French Revolution, when the royalty of France was in financial trouble, the king of France sought out such a clever banker, and appointed him to a high position. This man was, in every regard, the opposite of the people who, up to that time, had ruled France. First of all he was not a Frenchman, he was a foreigner—a Genevese. Secondly, he was not a member of the aristocracy, he was a simple commoner. And what counted even more in eighteenth century France, he was not a Catholic, but a Protestant. And so Monsieur Necker, the father of the famous Madame de Staël, became the minister of finance, and everyone expected him to solve the financial problems of France, but in spite of the high degree of confidence Monsieur Necker enjoyed, the royal cashbox remained empty—Necker's greatest mistake having been his attempt to finance aid to the American colonists in their war of independence against England *without raising taxes*. That was certainly the wrong way to go about solving France's financial troubles.

No Secret Source of Funds

There can be no secret way to the solution of the financial problems of a government; if it needs money, it has to obtain the money by taxing its citizens (or, under special conditions, by borrowing it from people who have the money). But many governments, we can even say *most* governments, think there is another method for getting the needed money; simply to print it.

If the government wants to do something beneficial—if, for example, it wants to build a hospital—the way to find the needed money for this project is to tax the citizens and build the hospital out of tax revenues. Then no special "price revolution" will occur, because when the government collects money for the construction of the hospital, the citizens—having paid the taxes—are forced to reduce their spending. The individual taxpayer is forced to restrict either his consumption, his investments or his savings. The government, appearing on the market as a buyer, *replaces* the individual citizen: the citizen buys less, but the government buys more. The government, of course, does not always buy the same goods which the citizens would have bought; but on the average there occurs no rise in prices due to the government's construction of a hospital.

I choose this example of a hospital precisely because people sometimes say: "It makes a difference whether the government uses its money for good or for bad purposes. I want to assume that the government *always* uses the money which it has printed for the best possible purposes— purposes with which we all agree. For it is not the *way* in which the money is spent, it is the way in which the government *obtains* this money that brings about those consequences we call inflation and which most people in the world today do not consider as beneficial.

For example, without inflating, the government could use the tax-collected money for hiring new employees or for raising the salaries of those who are already in government service. Then these people, whose salaries have been increased, are in a position to buy more. When the government taxes the citizens and uses this money to increase the salaries of government employees, the taxpayers have less to spend, but the government employees have more. Prices in general will not increase.

But if the government does not use tax money for this purpose, if it uses freshly printed money instead, it means that there will be people who now have more money while all other people still have as much as they had before. So those who received the newly printed money will be competing with those people who were buyers before. And since there are no more commodities than there were previously, but there is more money on the market—and since there are now people who can buy more today than they could have bought yesterday—there will be an additional demand for that same quantity of goods. Therefore prices will tend to go up. This cannot be avoided, no matter what the use of this newly issued money will be.

And most importantly, this tendency for prices to go up will develop step by step; it is not a general upward movement of what has been called the "price level." The metaphorical expression "price level" must never be used.

When people talk of a "price level," they have in mind the image of a level of a liquid which goes up or down according to the increase or decrease in its quantity, but which, like a liquid in a tank, always rises evenly. But with prices, there is no such thing as a "level." Prices do not change to the same extent at the same time. There are always prices that are changing more rapidly, rising or falling more rapidly than other prices. There is a reason for this.

Early Beneficiaries

Consider the case of the government employee who received the new money added to the money supply. People do not buy today precisely the same commodities and in the same quantities as they did yesterday. The additional money which the government has printed and introduced into the market is not used for the purchase of *all* commodities and services. It is used for the purchase of certain commodities, the prices of which will rise, while other commodities will still remain at the prices that prevailed before the new money was put on the market. Therefore, when inflation starts, different groups within the population are affected by this inflation, in different ways. Those groups who get the new money first, gain a temporary benefit.

When the government inflates in order to wage a war, it has to buy munitions, and the first to get the additional money are the munition industries and the workers within these industries. These groups are now in a very favorable position. They have higher profits and higher wages; their business is moving. Why? Because they were the first to receive the additional money. And having now more money at their disposal, they are buying. And they are buying from other people who are manufacturing and selling the commodities that these munition makers want.

These other people form a second group. And this second group considers inflation to be very good for business. Why not? Isn't it wonderful to sell more? For example, the owner of a restaurant in the neighborhood of a munitions factory says: "It is really marvelous! The munition workers have more money; there are many more of them now than before; they are all patronizing my restaurant; I am very happy about it." He does not see any reason to feel otherwise.

The situation is this: those people to whom the money comes first now have a higher income, and they can still buy many commodities and services at prices which correspond to the previous state of the market, to the condition that existed on the eve of inflation. Therefore, they are in a very favorable position. And thus inflation continues step by step, from one group of the population to another. And all those to whom the additional money comes at the early stage of inflation are benefited because they are buying some things at prices still corresponding to the previous stage of the exchange ratio between money and commodities.

Others Must Lose

But there are other groups in the population to whom this additional money comes much, much later. These people are in an *unfavorable* position. Before the additional money comes to them they are forced to pay higher prices than they paid before for some—or for practically all—of the commodities they wanted to purchase, while their income has remained the same, or has not increased proportionately with prices.

Consider for instance a country like the United States during the Second World War; on the one hand, inflation at that time favored the munitions workers, the munition industries, the manufacturers of guns, while on the other hand it worked against other groups of the population. And the ones who suffered the greatest disadvantages from inflation were the teachers and the ministers.

As you know, a minister is a very modest person who serves God and must not talk too much about money. Teachers, likewise, are dedicated persons who are supposed to think more about educating the young than about their salaries. Consequently, the teachers and ministers were among those who were most penalized by inflation, for the various schools and churches were the last to realize that they must raise salaries. When the church elders and the school corporations finally discovered that, after all one should also raise the salaries of those dedicated people, the earlier losses they had suffered still remained.

For a long time, they had to buy less than they did before, to cut down their consumption of better and more expensive foods, and to restrict their purchase of clothing—because prices had already adjusted upward, while their income, their salaries, had not yet been raised. (This situation has changed considerably today, at least for teachers.)

There are therefore always different groups in the population being affected differently by inflation. For some of them, inflation is not so bad;

they even ask for a continuation of it, because they are the first to profit from it. We will see, in the next lecture, how this unevenness in the consequences of inflation vitally affects the politics that lead toward inflation.

Under these changes brought about by inflation, we have groups who are favored and groups who are directly profiteering. I do not use the term "profiteering" as a reproach to these people, for if there is someone to blame, it is the government that established the inflation. And there are always people who *favor* inflation, because they realize what is going on sooner than other people do. Their special profits are due to the fact that there will necessarily be unevenness in the process of inflation.

Inflation as a Tax

The government may think that inflation—as a method of raising funds—is better than taxation, which is always unpopular and difficult. In many rich and great nations, legislators have often discussed, for months and months, the various forms of new taxes that were necessary because the parliament had decided to increase expenditures. Having discussed various methods of getting the money by taxation, they finally decided that perhaps it was better to do it by inflation.

But of course, the word "inflation" was not used. The politician in power who proceeds toward inflation does not announce: "I am proceeding toward inflation." The technical methods employed to achieve the inflation are so complicated that the average citizen does not realize inflation has begun.

During one of the biggest inflations in history, in the German Reich after the First World War, the inflation was not so momentous during the war. It was the inflation *after* the war that brought about the catastrophe. The government did not say: "We are proceeding toward inflation." The government simply borrowed money very indirectly from the central bank. The government did not have to ask how the central bank would find and deliver the money. The central bank simply printed it.

Today the techniques for inflation are complicated by the fact that there is checkbook money. It involves another technique, but the result is the same. With the stroke of a pen, the government creates *fiat* money, thus increasing the quantity of money and credit. The government simply issues the order, and the fiat money is there.

The government does not care, at first, that some people will be losers, it does not care that prices will go up. The legislators say: "This is a wonderful system!" But this wonderful system has one fundamental weakness: it cannot last. If inflation could go on forever, there would be no point in telling governments they should not inflate. But the certain fact about inflation is that, sooner or later, it must come to an end. It is a policy that cannot last.

In the long run, inflation comes to an end with the breakdown of the currency—to a catastrophe, to a situation like the one in Germany in 1923. On August 1, 1914, the value of the dollar was four *marks* and twenty *pfennigs*. Nine years and three months later, in November 1923, the dollar was pegged at 4.2 trillion *marks*. In other words, the *mark* was worth nothing. It no longer had *any* value.

Some years ago, a famous author wrote: "In the long run we are all dead." This is certainly true, I am sorry to say. But the question is, how short or long will the short run be? In the eighteenth century there was a famous lady, Madame de Pompadour, who is credited with the dictum: "Après nous le déluge" ("After us will come the flood"). Madame de Pompadour was happy enough to die in the short run. But her successor in office, Madame du Barry, outlived the short run and was beheaded in the long run. For many people the "long run" quickly becomes the "short run"—and the longer inflation goes on the sooner the "short run."

How long can the short run last? How long can a central bank continue an inflation? Probably as long as people are convinced that the government, sooner or later, but certainly not too late, will stop printing money and thereby stop decreasing the value of each unit of money.

The Flight from Money

When people no longer believe this, when they realize that the government will go on and on without any intention of stopping, then they begin to understand that prices tomorrow will be higher than they are today. Then they begin buying at any price, causing prices to go up to such heights that the monetary system breaks down.

I refer to the case of Germany, which the whole world was watching. Many books have described the events of that time. (Although I am no German, but an Austrian, I saw everything from the inside: in Austria, conditions were not very different from those in Germany; nor were they much different in many other European countries.) For several years, the German people believed that their inflation was just a temporary affair, that it would soon come to an end. They believed it for almost nine years, until the summer of 1923. Then, finally, they began to doubt. As the inflation continued, people thought it wiser to buy everything available, instead of keeping money in their pockets. Furthermore, they reasoned that one should not give loans of money, but on the contrary, that it was a very good idea to be a debtor. Thus inflation continued feeding on itself.

And it went on in Germany until exactly August 28, 1923. The masses had believed inflation money to be real money, but then they found out that conditions had changed. At the end of the German inflation, in the fall of 1923, the German factories paid their workers every morning in advance for the day. And the workingman who came to the factory with his wife, handed his wages—all the millions he got—over to her immediately. And the lady immediately went to a shop to buy something, no matter what. She realized what most people knew at that time—that overnight, from one day to another, the *mark* lost 50 percent of its purchasing power. Money, like chocolate on a hot oven, was melting in the pockets of the people. This last phase of German inflation did not last long; after a few days, the whole nightmare was over: the *mark* was valueless and a new currency had to be established.

Lord Keynes, the same man who said that in the long run we are all dead, was one of the long line of inflationist authors of the twentieth century. They all wrote against the gold standard. When Keynes attacked the gold standard, he called it a "barbarous relic." And most people today consider it ridiculous to speak of a return to the gold standard. In the United States, for instance, you are considered to be more or less a dreamer if you say: "Sooner or later, the United States will have to return to the gold standard."

Yet the gold standard has one tremendous virtue: the quantity of the money supply, under the gold standard, is independent of the policies of governments and political parties. This is its advantage. It is a form of protection against spendthrift governments. If, under the gold standard, a government is asked to spend money for something new, the minister of finance can say: "And where do I get the money? Tell me, first, how I will find the money for this additional expenditure."

A Restraint on Spending

Under an inflationary system, nothing is simpler for the politicians to do than to order the government printing office to provide as much money as they need for their projects. Under a gold standard, sound government has a much better chance; its leaders can say to the people and to the politicians: "We can't do it unless we increase taxes."

But under inflationary conditions, people acquire the habit of looking upon the government as an institution with limitless means at its disposal: the state, the government, can do anything. If, for instance, the nation wants a new highway system, the government is expected to build it. But where will the government get the money?

One could say that in the United States today—and even in the past, under McKinley—the Republican party was more or less in favor of sound money and of the gold standard, and the Democratic party was in favor of inflation. Of course not a paper inflation, but of silver.

It was, however, a Democratic president of the United States, President Cleveland, who at the end of the 1880s vetoed a decision of Congress, to give a small sum—about $10,000—to help a community that had suffered some disaster. And President Cleveland justified his veto by writing: "While it is the duty of the citizens to support the government, it is not the duty of the government to support the citizens." This is something which every statesman should write on the wall of his office to show to people who come asking for money.

I am rather embarrassed by the necessity to simplify these problems. There are so many complex problems in the monetary system, and I would not have written volumes about them if they were as simple as I am describing them here. But the fundamentals are precisely these: if you increase the quantity of money, you bring about the lowering of the purchasing power of the monetary unit. This is what people whose private affairs are unfavorably affected do not like. People who do not benefit from inflation are the ones who complain.

A Worldwide Plague

If inflation is bad and if people realize it, why has it become almost a way of life in all countries? Even some of the richest countries suffer from this disease. The United States today is certainly the richest country in the world, with the highest standard of living. But when you travel in the United States, you will discover that there is constant talk about inflation and about the necessity to stop it. But they only talk; they do not act.

To give you some facts: after the First World War, Great Britain returned to the prewar gold parity of the pound. That is, it revalued the pound upward. This increased the purchasing power of every worker's wages. In an unhampered market the nominal *money* wage would have fallen to compensate for this and the workers' *real* wage would not have suffered. We do not have time here to discuss the reasons for this. But the unions in Great Britain were unwilling to accept an adjustment of wage rates to the higher purchasing power of the monetary unit, therefore *real* wages were raised considerably by this monetary measure. This was a serious catastrophe for England, because Great Britain is a predominantly industrial country that has to import its raw materials, half-finished goods, and foodstuffs in order to live, and has to export manufactured goods to pay for these imports. With the rise in the international value of the pound, the price of British goods rose on foreign markets and sales and exports declined. Great Britain had, in effect, priced itself out of the world market.

The unions could not be defeated. You know the power of a union today. It has the right, practically the privilege, to resort to violence. And a union order is, therefore, let us say, not less important than a government decree. The government decree is an order for enforcement for which the enforcement apparatus of the government—the police—is ready. You must obey the government decree, otherwise you will have difficulties with the police.

The Impact of Unions

Unfortunately, we have now, in almost all countries all over the world, a second power that is in a position to exercise force: the labor unions. The labor unions determine wages and the strikes to enforce them in the same way in which the government might decree a minimum wage rate. I will not discuss the union question now; I shall deal with it later. I only want to establish that it is the union policy to raise wage rates *above* the level they would have on an unhampered market. As a result, a considerable part of the potential labor force can be employed only by people or industries that are prepared to suffer losses. And, since businesses are not able to keep on suffering losses, they close their doors and people become unemployed. The setting of wage rates above the level they would have on the unhampered market always results in the unemployment of a considerable part of the potential labor force.

In Great Britain, the result of high wage rates enforced by the labor unions was lasting unemployment, prolonged year after year. Millions of workers were unemployed, production figures dropped. Even experts were perplexed. In this situation the British government made a move which it considered an indispensable, emergency measure: it *devalued* its currency.

The result was that the purchasing power of the money wages, upon which the unions had insisted, was no longer the same. The *real* wages, the commodity wages, were reduced. Now the worker could not buy as much as he had been able to buy before, even though the nominal wage rates remained the same. In this way, it was thought, *real* wage rates would return to free market levels and unemployment would disappear.

This measure—devaluation—was adopted by various other countries, by France, the Netherlands, and Belgium. One country even resorted twice to this measure within a period of one year and a half. That country was Czechoslovakia. It was a surreptitious method, let us say, to thwart the power of the unions. You could not call it a real success, however.

Indexation

After a few years, the people, the workers, even the unions, began to understand what was going on. They came to realize that currency devaluation had reduced their real wages. The unions had the power to oppose this. In many countries they inserted a clause into wage contracts providing that money wages must go up automatically with an increase in prices. This is called *indexing*. The unions became index conscious. So, this method of reducing unemployment that the government of Great Britain started in 1931—which was later adopted by almost all important governments—this method of "solving unemployment" no longer works today.

In 1936, in his *General Theory of Employment, Interest and Money,* Lord Keynes unfortunately elevated this method—those emergency measures of the period between 1929 and 1933—to a *principle,* to a fundamental system of policy. And he justified it by saying, in effect: "Unemployment is bad. If you want unemployment to disappear you must inflate the currency."

He realized very well that wage rates can be too high for the market, that is, too high to make it profitable for an employer to increase his work force, thus too high from the point of view of the total working population, for with wage rates imposed by unions above the market level, only a part of those anxious to earn wages can obtain jobs.

And Keynes said, in effect: "Certainly mass unemployment, prolonged year after year, is a very unsatisfactory condition." But instead of suggesting that wage rates could and should be adjusted to market conditions, he said, in effect: "If one devalues the currency and the workers are not clever enough to realize it, they will not offer resistance against a drop in real wage rates, as long as nominal wage rates remain the same." In other words, Lord Keynes was saying that if a man gets the same amount of sterling today as he got before the currency was devalued, he will not realize that he is, in fact, now getting less.

In old-fashioned language, Keynes proposed cheating the workers. Instead of declaring openly that wage rates must be adjusted to the conditions of the market—because, if they are not, a part of the labor force will inevitably remain unemployed—he said, in effect: "Full employment can be reached only if you have inflation. Cheat the workers." The most interesting fact, however, is that when his *General Theory* was published, it was no longer possible to cheat, because people had already become index conscious. But the goal of full employment remained.

Full Employment

What does "full employment" mean? It has to do with the unhampered labor market, which is not manipulated by the union or by the government. On this market, wage rates for every type of labor tend to reach a level where everybody who wants a job can get one and every employer can hire as many workers as he needs. If there is an increase in the demand for labor, the wage rate will tend to be greater, and if fewer workers are needed, the wage rate will tend to fall.

The only method by which a "full employment" situation can be brought about is by the maintenance of an unhampered labor market. This is valid for every kind of labor and for every kind of commodity.

What does a businessman do who wants to sell a commodity for five dollars a unit? When he cannot sell it at that price, the technical business expression in the United States is, "the inventory does not move." But it *must* move. He cannot retain things because he must buy something new; fashions are changing. So he sells at a lower price. If he cannot sell the merchandise at five dollars, he must sell it at four. If he cannot sell it at four, he must sell it at three. There is no other choice as long as he stays in business. He may suffer losses, but these losses are due to the fact that his anticipation of the market for his product was wrong.

It is the same with the thousands and thousands of young people who come every day from the agricultural districts into the city, trying to earn money. It happens so in every industrial nation. In the United States they come to town with the idea that they should get, say, a hundred dollars a week. This may be impossible. So if a man cannot get a job for a hundred dollars a week, he must try to get a job for ninety or eighty dollars, and perhaps even less. But if he were to say—as the unions do—"one hundred dollars a week or nothing," then he might have to remain unemployed. (Many do not mind being unemployed, because the government pays unemployment benefits out of special taxes levied on the employers—which are sometimes nearly as high as the wages the man would receive if he were employed.)

Because a certain group of people believes that full employment can be attained only by inflation, inflation is accepted in the United States. But people are discussing the question: Should we have a sound currency with unemployment, or inflation with full employment? This is in fact a very vicious analysis.

Clarifying the Problem

To deal with this problem we must raise the question: How can one improve the condition of the workers and of all other groups of the population? The answer is: by maintaining an unhampered labor market and thus achieving full employment. Our dilemma is, shall the market determine wage rates or shall they be determined by union pressure and compulsion? The dilemma is *not* "shall we have inflation or unemployment?"

This mistaken analysis of the problem is argued in England, in European industrial countries, and even in the United States. And some people say: "Now look, even the United States is inflating. Why should we not do it also?"

To these people one should answer first of all: "One of the privileges of a rich man is that he can afford to be foolish much longer than a poor man." And this is the situation of the United States. The financial policy of the United States is very bad and is getting worse. Perhaps the United States can afford to be foolish a bit longer than some other countries.

The most important thing to remember is that inflation is not an act of God, that inflation is not a catastrophe of the elements or a disease that comes like a plague. Inflation is a *policy*—a deliberate policy of people who resort to inflation because they consider it to be a lesser evil than unemployment. But the fact is that, in the not very long run, inflation does *not* cure unemployment.

Inflation is a policy. And a policy can be changed. Therefore, there is no reason to give in to inflation. If one regards inflation as an evil, then one has to stop inflating. One has to balance the budget of the government. Of course, public opinion must support this; the intellectuals must help the people to understand. Given the support of public opinion, it is certainly possible for the people's elected representatives to abandon the policy of inflation.

We must remember that, in the long run, we may all be dead and certainly will be dead. But we should arrange our earthly affairs, for the short run in which we have to live, in the best possible way. And one of the measures necessary for this purpose is to abandon inflationary policies.

Inflation

by F. A. Harper

Inflation can be prevented. Failure to do so is purely and simply a matter of negligence.

Inflation is a trick done with money. Suppose that the government were to provide vending machines all over the country where persons could deposit each dollar they now have and get two in return, by merely pressing a button. If everyone were to use this gadget, each person could then pay twice as much as before for everything he buys. That would be inflation in a clear and simple form.

People could, of course, put away some of this new money in "a sock" or otherwise hide it from circulation and use. But with this inflation gadget operating, there would be less incentive than before to keep the money in hiding, because it would become worth less and less with passing time. So the hoarding of money isn't likely to solve the present inflation problem, if it persists.

Inflation means too much money. The way to prevent inflation, then, is to close down the money factory. It is just that simple.

All the complicated gibberish one hears and reads about inflation simply blocks an understanding of the essentials of the problem—though it may impress the ignorant, or hide the negligence of those who are responsible for inflation by making the task of preventing inflation seem hopelessly complicated.

The Money Factory

Where is the money factory? Who operates it?

The money factory in our present money system is operated by the federal government, either directly or by farming it out to subcontractors under the control of government. It makes paper money to replace that

The late Dr. Harper, long a member of the staff of the Foundation for Economic Education, was founder and president of the Institute for Humane Studies. This article, slightly condensed from his pamphlet first published in 1951, appeared in the November 1967 issue of *The Freeman*.

which has become dirty or worn out. It makes new paper money to increase the supply. It makes pennies, nickels, and the other coins. It permits the banks to grant credit to borrowers, which becomes money that is interchangeable with any of the other forms of money in use.

But for purposes of seeing where responsibility lies in the inflation problem, we need not concern ourselves with all these different kinds of money. It is necessary only to say that at present all forms of money come out of the government factory, or are controlled by the government, under a complete monopoly.

If anyone doubts the existence of this money monopoly by the government, he can test it by manufacturing some money himself—even one cent. He would then be charged with counterfeiting, and be given a penitentiary sentence for having infringed on the monopoly. The policeman in this instance is the one who holds the monopoly.

The money monopoly is a strange one. We usually think of a monopoly as restricting output, which can then be sold at a much higher price. But in the money monopoly, the government can force the citizens to take the entire output of its product.

A Highly Profitable Monopoly

Not only that, but the operation is highly profitable—nearly 100 percent, or almost the entire price of the product. This is one clear case of an "excess profit" which the victimized customers are forced to pay.

If the money monopoly were not so profitable, there would be no inflation problem at this time. The profit incentive works with money and stimulates its production, just as it does with anything else. In olden days when some otherwise useful commodity like gold, for instance, was used as money, anyone who wished could produce as much of it as he liked. The production of money was then legal and competitive, rather than being a crime as it is now. Its production was so costly in time and expense that the inefficient producers were crowded out, just as they are crowded out of the production of brooms or mousetraps.

But it is not so with present-day money, with the paper bills and deposits that make up most of our money of exchange. It doesn't cost much for the paper and ink and printing needed to make a $100 bill. It is probably the most profitable monopoly that ever existed, and the entire force of the federal government is available to protect its monopoly against the infringement of private counterfeiting.

When a private citizen counterfeits money, the wrath of other citizens is aroused and they say: "He did no useful work to get that money, and yet he spends it in the marketplace, taking food, clothing, and other things away from those of us who have earned our money by working for it. He takes useful things out of the market without producing other useful things to go into the market, as we do. The effect of his chicanery is that prices go up and the rest of us receive less and less for our money."

This is a correct statement of what happens under counterfeiting. It is the reason for objecting to counterfeiting, because the counterfeiter gets something for nothing. And it is the reason for objecting to legal counterfeiting, too. If everybody tried to live off counterfeit money, one would at once discover its effect in the extreme. There would be nothing to buy with the money and it would be completely worthless.

When the government makes new money and spends it, the effect on the supply of things in the market to be bought by civilians with their earnings, and the effect on prices, is exactly the same as when any private counterfeiter does so. The only difference between the two is whether it is a private counterfeiter that gets benefits looted from others, or whether it is a counterfeiting government spending it on pet projects—projects that the citizens are unwilling to finance either by private investment or by tax payments.

The Watered Punch

Counterfeit money affects what you can get for your money in the market much like water affects the punch at a bring-your-own party. Each in attendance is to be allowed to dip into the punch bowl in proportion to the quantity of ingredients he has brought and dumped into it. All bring some pure ingredient wanted in the mixture.

Now suppose that one person brings water, and dumps it in. This dilutes the punch, but the person who does it is permitted to drink of the mixture the same as those who are being cheated. He gets something for nothing, and the rest get nothing for something by an equal amount. If everyone were to do the same as he has done, it would be perfectly clear what the adding of water does to the taste of the punch. So it is with counterfeit money, whether done privately or by the government.

Why Government Inflates Money

The government makes this new money in order to cover what it spends in excess of its income—its costs in excess of its tax revenues. The government makes up the shortage with the new money made in its monopolistic money factory. For our present purposes, it makes no difference whether this is done with paper bills directly, or with bills which it obtains by issuing another form of paper money—government bonds—which are forced upon the banking system.

What the government does is like a counterfeiter who continuously spends more than his earnings, and who goes to his basement print shop each evening and makes enough counterfeit money to balance the shortage. His print shop might put out either paper money direct, or counterfeit bonds which he sells to the banks in exchange for the money; the effect would be the same in either instance.

Living Within Income

The way—the only way—to stop this form of inflation is for the government to live within its income. This can be done either by raising enough in taxes to meet its costs, or by paring down its costs to equal its income.

In a family, the housewife may try the former method—nudging the husband to ask for a raise, or to hustle for more sales—but in the end the family must always resolve the problem by spending less than it would like to spend, and living within its income.

The government holds unlimited power to tax every family in the nation, and for decades has been raising more and more taxes, but it has never resolved the problem that way. It appears to have forgotten the possibility of reducing expenses as the means of living within its income and avoiding inflation. So we have had inflation almost continuously since 1931, and are now faced with its acceleration.

The only way to prevent inflation is to prevent these governmental deficits; to pay currently and in full all the expenses of government that we either demand or tolerate. To do this it is necessary either to increase taxes or to cut down the costs of government. We are only kidding ourselves if we say that we can avoid both taxes and governmental frugality, by inflation-financing of the excess of its costs over its income.

Inflation a Form of Tax

Inflation of the type we are discussing is in reality a form of tax, not an alternative to taxes. It is, in fact, perhaps the most pernicious form of tax, for the reason that it is not recognized as such. It can ply its evil way under cover of this ignorance, and without the resistances and disciplines of a tax that is open and recognized.

We speak of direct and indirect taxes. Property taxes or income taxes which are paid by individuals are direct taxes; only about one-third of all taxes are of this type where we can see them clearly. Indirect taxes, making up the other two-thirds, are collected at some point away from the consumer, and become buried in the prices of the things we buy and the services we employ. All these direct and indirect taxes are at specific rates which are set by a governmental body charged with that responsibility. They decide what will be taxed, and how much.

But with inflation, which is in reality also a tax, it is not these taxing bodies which designate the tax. It is a tax created by default. When the spending part of government outruns the taxing part, the difference is financed by governmental counterfeit, by inflation which falls as a tax on each person in the marketplace in the form of higher prices for what he buys. Everyone who uses money for buying in the market pays some of this form of tax. It is the close equivalent of a sales tax on everything. One who favors deficit spending—the inflation tax—should not be opposed to a sales tax imposed on all purchases of goods and services, without exception. The only important difference is that the sales tax is known to be a tax, but the inflation-tax is thought to be avoidance or postponement of the tax.

Postponed Taxes a Myth

This makes clear, I believe, why inflation is such a pernicious form of tax. People who would otherwise protest and curb the extravagances of government are lulled by the foolish notion that inflation is a means of postponing payment of some of the current costs of government.

It is especially tempting to try to avoid taxes when the government is spending with abandon for a "national emergency." It is then argued that "since the expensive projects of government are largely for the benefit of later generations," why shouldn't part of the costs be left for them to pay? This notion, as has been said, has become a steady habit in the United States.

The truth is, however, that if the government this year dips into the national punch bowl of goods and services that are produced and available, what it takes out and squanders this year is not there for others this year. The more government takes and squanders this year, the less someone will get back this year compared with what he produces.

Why, if we ignore the minor item of foreign trade balances, is it believed that a nation can postpone this year's cost of government? Probably it is the presence of money that confuses us. If we were to think only of punch and potatoes and things—exchanged by barter—we would not be confused, because we would then realize that we cannot eat potatoes this year which are to be grown next year.

A whole nation of persons can't go on year after year consuming more than it has to consume. It can't do it for one year, or even for one day. It can't do it by allowing inflation, or by any other means. Failure to realize that inflation is a form of tax leads to the false belief that inflation affords a means of postponing some of the costs of government. But it can't be done.

If it were possible for a whole nation to postpone one-third of this year's cost of government until next year, why not postpone half of it? All of it? And if it is possible to postpone it until next year, why not postpone it for two years? Ten? Forever? If this were possible, we would not need to wait for utopia. We could have it now!

Government Fights Government: The Inflation Fighters

Our present situation comes into clearer focus when it is realized that inflation is a form of tax. A part of the costs of government are paid for by what is commonly called taxes, in both direct and hidden forms, levied by the taxing part of government. The remainder of the costs of government is paid for by the inflation-tax, which is in reality levied by the appropriations part of government over the protest of the taxing part of government, which has refused to raise all the taxes needed to cover all appropriations. This results in inflation, and prices rise.

There then is said to arise "need" for another big project in government, the "inflation fighters." A big force of lawyers, economists, and policemen are hired.

They organize the citizens into community inflation-fighting gangs, to lend an appearance of local respectability to the endeavor. These local organizations also insure that neighbors will be enrolled to serve as policemen over their neighbors, in the front line trenches where the fiercest fighting is most likely to occur.

Why does all this new machinery seem to be necessary? What are they doing? The new branch of government is set up for the purpose of fighting the payment of the inflation-tax that has been assessed by another branch of government—the appropriations division. It would be as logical to have the government set up a big unit in Washington, with citizens committees and all that, to conduct a tax revolt against the payment of income taxes—to fight the Internal Revenue branch of the Treasury Department.

Economic Quackery

Every illusion floats on a plausibility.

Quack medical doctors attack the most vivid symptom with something that is plausible to the suffering patient. The treatment may be to throw cold water on a fevered patient, or to throw hot water on one with chills. The quack doctor may use two thermometers—one that does not rise above 98.6 degrees which he uses for fever patients, and another that does not fall below that point which he uses for chill patients—to "prove" that his "cure" has been effective.

A quack engineer might try to prevent an explosion by adjusting the pressure gauge downward or closing the safety valve. Or a quack railroad engineer might try to prevent a wreck by adjusting the speed gauge downward instead of reducing the speed.

All these are silly, indeed, but no more silly than their equivalents in the economic field. "Price control to prevent inflation" is also silly. The only reason why the medical plausibilities seem more silly than these economic ones is that medicine is further advanced and more widely understood. The economic mistakes we are now bringing upon ourselves may one day appear to our descendants to be just as foolish as the medical superstitions of old now appear to us.

Freezing the Price Thermometer

When there is inflation, prices rise. It would appear, then, that inflation is caused by rising prices. And this is the weapon of plausibility selected by the price-control part of government to justify its fight against the appropriations part: "The way to fight inflation is simple—just establish price controls, and prohibit prices from rising."

There are two ways, in general, to test the truth of a proposal like this, and to prevent the practice of quackery: (1) judging from experience, and (2) reasoning to the right answer. By both of these tests, price control is shown to be economic quackery.

Lessons from History

There has been a wealth of historical experience with price controls. In fact, a recent archaeological discovery reveals that the oldest known laws in the world were price control laws—3,800 years ago in ancient Babylonia.

One of the best summaries of historical experience with price controls is easily accessible to governmental officials and others. In 1922, Mary G. Lacy, Librarian of the government's Bureau of Agricultural Economics, addressed the Agricultural History Society under the title: "Food Control During Forty-six Centuries." She pointed out how her search of history over this entire period revealed repeated attempts in many nations to curb by law the inflationary rises of price. She said:

> The results have been astonishingly uniform . . . . The history of government limitation of price seems to teach one clear lesson: That in attempting to ease the burdens of the people in a time of high prices by artificially setting a limit to them, the people are not relieved but only exchange one set of ills for another which is greater...The man, or class of men, who controls the supply of essential foods is in possession of supreme power . . . . They had to exercise this control in order to hold supreme power, because all the people need food and it is the only commodity of which this is true.

But we need not go so far back into history, and to a foreign land, for evidence. During World War II we were experiencing some of the vivid consequences of these controls in the form of the "meat famine." It was not a true shortage of meat at all. The trouble was that controls were preventing its exchange, all along the lines of trade from producer to consumer. This was only one small sample of the consequences of those wartime controls. How short are our memories?

Free Price Is Economic Governor

Some may be tempted to ignore this long history of failure of price controls on grounds that "conditions are now different." Then they evidently do not understand the reasons why price controls must always fail. These reasons are perhaps the best test of whether they are likely to fail of their avowed purpose this time.

It is impossible to consume something that has not been produced, and it is foolish to produce something that is not going to be consumed—to throw it away, or let it rot. It follows, then, that a balance between what is produced and what is consumed is the most desirable condition—if, in fact, it is not economically imperative to have this balance. How is this balance of "supply" and "demand" to be attained?

Under a condition of price freedom, those who produce and those who consume will resolve this problem peacefully. The means by which they do it can best be visualized by the use of a chart, simplified for purposes of illustration. The details, shown here as equal changes in price and quantities, differ from one product or service to another and change with passing time. But despite these differences, the principles we shall derive apply to each product; and they apply whether the price is controlled directly by government or by any other form of monopoly.

These are the principles of price—free and controlled:

1. Reductions in price cause increases in the quantities wanted.
2. Reductions in price cause decreases in the quantities offered.
3. Supply and demand are equal at only one point—the free market price; higher prices always cause surpluses; lower prices always cause shortages.

4. Trading and the economic welfare of both producers and consumers are greatest at the free market price, and are prevented as prices are forced either higher or lower.

The only instance in which "price fixing" fails to have these consequences is where it is set at the free market level, in which event the governmental edict is a sham because that is where the price would be in the absence of this pointless edict. This is the point where people are freely acting in response to the inexorable signals of the market place. Yet, doing business at this price becomes "lawlessness" and "irresponsibility" by edict when price control sets it elsewhere.

Prices that are rigged very high or very low will kill off practically all trading. Attempts to stimulate production, consumption, and trading by forced labor, socializing of property, and subsidies to producers and consumers are all awkward attempts to replace the performance of people in a free market.

Under controls, those near the source of supply get most of it, and those at a distance have to go without. Black markets spring up. Distant consumers try to get some of the supply. Confusion increases and tempers mount. More and more price policemen are hired who, instead of producing useful things, try to quell the confusion and chaos. The bill for their salaries and other costs is sent to the unfortunate victims of the controls.

Will price control stop inflation? All history has shown it to have failed. There is only one point of price where supply and demand are in balance, where both shortage and surplus are avoided, where trade is most peaceful, and where welfare is at a maximum. If this incontestable fact is understood, the belief that we can escape reality by enacting price control laws must be dispelled as an illusion.

From Price Lies to Rationing

Price control really means that laws are passed to make official prices tell lies. One of the penalties for the lying is the creation of shortages that cannot be peacefully resolved.

The shortage, once created, must be dealt with by further powers of government and law. There must be "rationing"—rationing by the government of the shortage it has created by law, rationing of goods and services to individuals because the government failed to limit the output of its money factory.

When the free market is allowed to operate and to set the price at a point where supply and demand will equate, each person will have purchase tickets in the market which correspond to the supply of something he puts into the market. Gifts, of course, are an exception; but in the case of gifts, the rights to draw on the market are still given by the person who supplied the market with something to be bought. These purchase rights are tickets of merit based on production. And the whole thing balances out, as we have said, peacefully.

When the government intervenes with price control laws, this balance is no longer maintained. There are now more tickets for things than there are things to redeem. There are shortages created by law. Then governmental rationing seems to be needed, whereby government officials are empowered to decide who shall get the short supplies. This substitutes political considerations for the merit of production under a free price in a free market.

Laws That Promote Dishonesty

Not only do government-controlled prices lie, but the process also rapidly promotes dishonesty among all groups—merchants, producers, consumers, government employees, everybody. The temptation of bribery of government officials becomes great. Late during World War II, a grocer of extremely high integrity and wide experience, told me that it was absolutely impossible for anyone to practice honesty according to the law and still stay in that business under price controls. The reason for this should be clear when we consider the legislated falseness and interference with business operations that become involved.

If this nation is to carry a role of moral leadership in the world, it will have to be founded on the morality of individual persons. And this is destroyed by such laws.

The shortages that result from price and wage controls are purely a legal creation, created by the price control law and nothing else. *In an otherwise free economy, the "success" of any price control law can be measured by the extent of the shortage it creates, or the decline in production which it causes. And if such controls were complete and effec-*

tive, they would probably stop all production for trade, which uses money.
This conclusion is inescapable.

Under present conditions of inflation, caused by rampant governmental spending—with laws aimed at the symptoms of inflation rather than dealing with its cause—the time is short for making an important choice. Its nature is indicated by what Lenin allegedly said in 1924: "Some day we shall force the United States to spend itself into destruction." And Lord Keynes reports: "Lenin is said to have declared that the best way to destroy the Capitalist System was to debauch the currency. By a continuing process of inflation, governments can confiscate, secretly and unobserved, an important part of the wealth of their citizens." Lenin probably knew that price and other controls—one of the main objectives of the system he favored—would then be imposed.

Unless the price control law is rescinded, its disrupting influence will lead to governmental enslavement of all labor and confiscation of all production facilities—to adopt, in other words, a completely socialist-communist system which we are presumably opposing.

A Strange Dilemma: Lawlessness or Socialism

The only escape from the consequences of these laws would seem to be for the citizens to ignore them. This means lawlessness, technically, in the form of black market operations and all the other forms of evasion. This places the honest citizen who favors human liberty in a strange dilemma. He must choose between practicing lawlessness in this technical sense, or supporting a socialist-communist regime.

If we add to a moral breakdown of the people, the confusion that is created when illusions and wishful thinking bump up against economic laws which cannot be revoked by man-made laws, and add to this the animosity that grows under these conditions and the utter distrust of one another that is aroused, then the prospect is too sobering to be ignored.

A step in the direction of taking away the government's monopoly in the production of money, and restricting government to the judicial aspects of exchange, would be to compel the government to live within its income. This means limiting government expenditures, strictly and absolutely, to taxes that are openly acknowledged to be taxes. It means prohibition of the concealed and deceptive tax of inflation.

If this were to be done, there no longer would be an inflation problem of the type we now have. If this were to be done, there no longer would be any excuse for the enactment of socialist-communist measures—these deceptive processes of legalized price fictions and interference with exchange. If this were to be done, it no longer would be "necessary" to give up our liberty under futile controls aimed at the consequences of inflation rather than at its cause.

Ruthless measures are called for after the citizens have allowed their servant—government—to become their master. But it is better to be ruthless and successful in preventing inflation than to become the victims of both ruthlessness and failure.

The Tragedy of Inflation: Much More than Higher Prices

by Bettina Bien Greaves

Inflation is very unpopular today. However, most who deplore it think of it simply as rising prices. But prices of goods and services may rise for many reasons: shortages due to destruction by pests, drought, flood, or increased demands when fashions change or a war breaks out. Thus, to define inflation as rising prices is far from helpful. In fact, it leads to serious error by directing attention to individuals who raise specific prices (businessmen) and wages (workers).

This definition of inflation neglects the real cause of generally rising prices—an increase in the quantity of money and/or credit. Once inflation is defined as monetary expansion, it becomes clear that only the government and government-privileged banks can be responsible. Only they may print money and/or create new dollar credit. Anyone else who tried to do so would be branded a counterfeiter.

Inflation, by which we mean monetary expansion, may proceed in several ways. The government may spend more money than it collects in taxes or borrows from individuals, filling the deficit (a) by printing paper money, or (b) by borrowing, through the Federal Reserve Banking system, new money or bank credit created by the "Fed" for this express purpose.

With the sanction, active encouragement and protection of government, private commercial banks may also increase the quantity of money by lending many times as much as the sums deposited by their customers in checking accounts. Commercial and savings banks are also able to expand the quantity of money and credit by an even greater ratio on the basis of savings and time deposits. Thus, the creation of new money, permitted and encouraged by government and government-promoted Federal Reserve policy, builds on itself and the number of dollars snowballs. Only

Mrs. Greaves is Associate Editor of *The Freeman* and Resident Scholar at FEE. She is currently working on the second volume of an annotated bibliography of works by and about Ludwig von Mises. This article appeared in the October 1981 issue of *The Freeman*.

by defining inflation as monetary expansion may we understand its more complex and far-ranging consequences.

A great deal has been written about the pressures produced on prices by a monetary expansion, shoving prices inevitably upward in an irregular and ragged fashion. Some prices are affected sooner, others later, some more, others less. Prices are not all affected equally, or proportionately to the monetary expansion. Because the effect of inflation on prices is uneven, its other consequences are serious, long-lasting and irreversible. It is these other consequences of inflation which we shall be considering here, consequences which make conditions worse, even from the point of view of the backers of the programs resulting in monetary expansion.

Some Win: Others Lose

There is no way to issue new dollars or bank credit so that everyone will benefit equally and simultaneously. Some politically favored persons always receive the newly-created money and bank credit sooner than others. Having more money gives these people a decided advantage in making purchases. They may buy more than they could have before. Or they may offer higher prices for what they want. Thus they can outbid other would-be purchasers who find less in the stores to buy at previously prevailing prices. Stocks of what the other would-be buyers would have purchased have been bought up by the new dollar holders. In this way, the first recipients of the new money "win," but always at the expense of others.

In time the new money will work its way through the market, from the first beneficiaries to those from whom they buy—merchants, suppliers, and so on—as each in turn receives some of the new dollars. But at each step in this sequence of transactions the advantage of having more dollars sooner than others is watered down a bit. Many who receive some of the new money much later will find they must pay higher prices without higher incomes. Thus inevitably those who receive some of the new money considerably later, or receive none at all, will lose.

Each transfer of dollars represents an irreversible shift of goods, services, wealth, and income. The "winners" gain at the permanent expense of the "losers." Although the losers are never easy to identify, their loss is real enough. They must struggle to adjust to a market in which the things they want are increasingly scarce and more expensive. Circumstances will change, of course. Attempts may be made to reverse the respective roles of "winners" and "losers." But compensation after the fact can never undo the harm done earlier. It can only set in operation a similar sequence of uneven, irregular, and ragged price shifts, creating different winners and losers.

Illusory Profits

Anyone whose selling prices are boosted by the issue of new dollars receives an unanticipated surplus. He gains due to the inflation. But this gain may not be a *real* gain. His increased income pushes him into a higher tax bracket. Then government promptly takes a greater portion than before. He may also have to pay higher prices to replace merchandise bought by the inflation-created "winners."

In anticipation of increased sales, merchants may order more of the particular items the new dollar holders are demanding. To fill these bigger orders, suppliers must also change their plans. To speed up or expand production of these particular commodities, they will have to offer more money to workers and to the owners of needed resources. Thus, the new dollars are passed further along throughout the economy, pushing up one wage here, another there, one price here, another there, and so on, adding to business costs along the line and reducing the gain merchants, suppliers, and producers had received from the inflation and on which they had paid taxes.

As a result of the inflation, enterprisers will also discover that the funds set aside for depreciation are insufficient to replace their equipment when it is worn out. With prices rising throughout the economy, new plants and new machinery, like almost everything else, cost more than before. Funds just aren't available for replacing them. If enterprisers are to continue operating, they must buy their new equipment out of either (a) current income or (b) borrowed funds. If they supplement insufficient depreciation allowances from current income, they will be using funds they should be accumulating to maintain their investment in the future, thus putting their enterprise in jeopardy. If they borrow additional funds from the banks, they will be helping to push interest rates up, thus increasing their business costs still more and further reducing their gain.

In time, what looks like an enterpriser's gain in dollar terms may be no gain at all. Receipts that seem exceptionally high in depreciating dollars are thus deceptive. It is extremely difficult to keep operating and maintain a profitable business during an inflation. If enterprisers fail to recognize that a dollar profit may be an illusory profit, if they fail to take this into consideration in planning, calculating, and allowing for depreciation, they will soon suffer losses that are *not* illusory but real! Yet through it all their books could still show dollar "profits," deceiving them into believing their enterprises are financially sound. "Illusory profits" may easily lure them into spending more than they can afford and consuming capital they cannot replace. Thus "profits" in terms of inflation-depreciated dollars mislead many an enterprise past the point of no return, down the road to bankruptcy.

Production Patterns Shifted

The new dollar holders spend their money for whatever they want most. If the new money goes first as benefits to unemployed workers or welfare recipients for instance, or as higher salaries to government employees, teachers, postmen, soldiers, and so on, it will probably be spent on consumer goods. If the new money goes first as loans to new car buyers and homeowners, it will be transferred to car salesmen, automobile workers, carpenters, electricians, and the like. If the new money goes first as bank credit to producers—builders, farmers, ship owners, automobile manufacturers, producers of military weapons, owners of radio and TV stations, and so on—it will probably go next to those who build tools, machines, factories, electronic equipment, and the like, and then later to those who extract and transport raw materials and other resources.

In any event, those who sell to the "winners" promptly enjoy an unexpected "boom" in that phase of their business. When they place orders with their suppliers to refill exhausted inventories of those particular items, the pattern of production starts to shift toward producing more of the things requested by the new-dollar spenders and less of what was being produced before. Step by step, producers respond to the demands of the new-dollar holders and those who receive the new-dollars.

As resources, capital, labor and energy shift production to satisfy the demands of the inflation "winners," the wants of the inflation "losers" are neglected. Those who receive none of the new money, or do not receive any until much later, are at a serious disadvantage in making purchases. They find in the stores fewer of the things they want to buy, because the "winners" bought more; they also find that prices are higher though their incomes are not. Moreover, the resources, capital, labor and energy which were used in producing for the politically-favored "winners" are no longer available, having been transformed into specialized tools and machines for supplying an artificial, government-subsidized market.

Malinvestment

If the monetary expansion is not halted, enterprisers will continue making adjustments to serve the consumer wants of new-dollar holders. Some enterprisers will turn next to making tools and machines for their production and others will seek to expand the supplies of the needed raw materials. Under our monetary system, the banks are encouraged by government policy to supply a large part of the funds needed to make shifts in production possible. They issue new credit through bank loans, creating additional dollars in the process, enabling the favored borrowers to spend more than before. But no more resources are available. The borrowers of the new credit must compete with other enterprisers for the available supplies. They soon discover that to hire additional workers and to buy more raw materials and tools and machines for their new projects, they must offer higher prices. Thus as they seek to fulfill their plans, they help to pass the new-dollars along in the form of rising prices. In time the patterns of prices and of production will deviate more and more from what they would have been in the absence of inflation.

In this world of ours, change is inevitable. It is the role of enterprisers to watch the market closely and to try to adjust to new conditions. If they succeed they make profits; if they fail, losses. What people are buying and refusing to buy at various prices gives producers and would-be producers important clues as to *what* to make and *how much* to make.

Clusters of Errors

Enterprisers sometimes misjudge the market and miscalculate consumer wants. On a free market, the mistakes of some enterprisers are usually counteracted, at least in part, by the correct judgments and successful calculations of others. But when government is introducing new-dollars and/or encouraging the banks to expand credit, most enterprisers are influenced by the same misleading factor—the expectation of continuing monetary expansion. Many enterprisers, misled by the inflation, shift production in the same direction. "Clusters of errors" appear.

Throughout the monetary expansion, producers are committing themselves and their resources more and more irretrievably to their various projects. Their investments become more specialized and less easily convertible to other uses. The longer the monetary expansion continues the greater the deviation from free market production and the more malinvestment occurs.

Inflation-instigated markets are notoriously unreliable. Government policy inevitably vacillates in response to the changing political climate. Without warning, the quantity of money and credit may be increased or decreased—political favors shifted. Once the flow of new-dollars and/or cheap credit declines or is halted, inflation-induced demands cannot be sustained. At one moment enterprisers are spurred to expand production in one direction. Then a shift in government policy leads unexpectedly to a drop in demand for their products. The market on which they had counted declines or disappears. They have produced too much of some things, not enough of others.

Mountains of Waste

When the inflation is slowed down or stopped, some consumer goods produced but not yet consumed may be sold to other customers. But many of the items intended for previously subsidized consumers cannot be sold for more than their inflation-boosted costs. Factories, tools, and machines, which cannot be converted to other uses, will be abandoned. Thus, the sooner inflation can be stopped the better, for the longer it continues, misdirecting production, the more resources will have been wasted and lost to future generations.

The vacillations of government intervention exaggerate the uncertainties of doing business. As the money spigot is turned on at one moment and off the next, many enterprisers swing back and forth between eagerness and reluctance in making commitments. In this way, the stops/goes, ons/offs of government interference lead in time to the ups and downs of business, the boom/bust sequence of the "trade cycle."

However, economic suffering cannot be avoided by continuing to inflate. For if monetary expansion is not halted, it must lead in time to a complete breakdown of the money and the market. If the inflation goes on until the monetary unit becomes worthless, business will come to a stand-still. With no reliable medium of exchange, no trades except simple barter deals can be made. Inflation-induced investments will fall into unemployment or serious *under*employment. Economic calculations, contractual agreements and production plans of any complexity will become impossible. Even those who, with the best of intentions, advocated the government programs that led to inflation must consider such conditions worse than those they were trying to improve.

Saving Discouraged

Saving is the principal source of increasing production. Only as people save can they have spare time and energy to devote to pleasure, learning new skills or developing and improving their tools, so as to be able to produce and have more tomorrow. It is out of savings that students may eat while acquiring knowledge and new skills. It is out of savings that inventors may live while devoting time to developing and producing new tools. It is out of savings too that workers and investors may survive while producing things for others to consume.

Most of what we have and enjoy in the world today—the many modern conveniences, complex tools and machines, remarkably efficient means of transportation, specialized electronic equipment, almost miraculous medical developments, and so on—we owe to past savers who set something aside out of what they produced and invested it in production. Thus our ancestors contributed to present-day living standards.

Our ancestors saved out of the desire to try to improve their productivity, to become financially independent and beholden to no one, to provide for themselves in old age, to care for their families in emergencies, and to improve conditions for their children and their children's children. The greater their confidence that savings and property would be fairly safe, the more incentive they had to forgo some immediate consumption for the sake of their own and their families' future welfare. Their savings and investments also helped support others while learning new skills, developing new technologies, inventing new machines and producing new factories. Thus their savings and investments are still contributing to our welfare today.

But our living standards are now in jeopardy. To meet the rising costs of government's rapidly increasing handouts, it increased taxes and resorted to inflation, both of which discourage saving. Fearful of losing their property and savings through inflation, producers have little incentive to save and invest in production. With less saved and invested, less is produced. With less produced, there is less to consume or to save and to invest. With less saved and invested today, there will be less for future generations to enjoy tomorrow.

Conclusion: Prolonged Inflation Means Economic Disaster

In summary, generally rising prices are one consequence of inflation, but by no means the most serious. Monetary expansion's other consequences are more destructive, long-lasting, and irreversible. It leads to injustices. Some persons win at the expense of others who "lose," never to be fully compensated for their inflation losses. Production is misdirected so that scarce resources are wasted on unwanted enterprises. "Illusory profits" deceive producers into economic miscalculations, malinvestments, and capital consumption, often placing their operations in jeopardy and perhaps forcing them into bankruptcy. Inflation adds to the uncertainties of doing business. Expansionist monetary policy is to blame for fostering unhealthy economic booms based on artificially stimulated malinvestments.

When political policies shift, artificial boom turns to economic bust with widespread economic losses and unemployment. Future generations will be poorer because inflation and credit expansion are discouraging saving and investment today. Inflation and credit expansion also discourage respect for private property, individual effort, and family responsibility. Why work for a living if the government is handing out benefits? Why save if every dollar loses purchasing power from day to day? Why invest in production if earnings are penalized by steeply rising taxes? Why strive for economic and family independence if there is no disgrace in benefiting from the wealth of others, taken from them by force through taxes and inflation?

Many malinvestments undoubtedly exist today due to past monetary expansion. However, the economic suffering such malinvestments bring about could be kept to the minimum if government were to renounce all further inflation and credit expansion immediately, not just try to slow them down. Left to their own devices, enterprisers would find ways in time to absorb and/or pass over and beyond most past losses and malinvestments. Confident that their economic calculations would not be upset by a depreciating currency, erratically rising prices, and illusory profits, they could return to producing goods and services for a non-artificial market. They would then be willing once more to save and invest, thus improving conditions for themselves, their families, and future generations.

But if government continues to offer benefits to some at the expense of others, financing them through higher taxes and monetary expansion, serious economic disaster must be expected. New evidence will then demonstrate once more the truth of Ludwig von Mises' statement that government interference with the economy, no matter how well intentioned, "produces results contrary to its purpose, that it makes conditions worse, not better, from the point of view of the government and those backing its interference."

Inflation Versus Employment

by Henry Hazlitt

For many years it has been popularly assumed that inflation increases employment. This belief has rested both on naive and on more sophisticated grounds.

The naive belief goes like this: When more money is printed, people have more "purchasing power"; they buy more goods, and employers take on more workers to make more goods.

The more sophisticated view was expounded by Irving Fisher in 1926:

> When the dollar is losing value, or in other words when the price level is rising, a businessman finds his receipts rising as fast, on the average, as this general rise of prices, but not his expenses, because his expenses consist, to a large extent, of things which are contractually fixed....Employment is then stimulated—for a time at least.[1]

This view contained a kernel of truth. But 32 years later, in 1958, the British economist A.W. Phillips published an article[2] which seemed to show that over the preceding century, when money-wage-rates rose, employment rose, and vice versa.

This, too, seemed a plausible relationship. Given a period for the most part noninflationary, but in which capital investment and invention were raising the unit-productivity of labor, profit margins on employment would be rising, in some years much more than in others; and in these years the demand for labor would increase, and employers would bid up wage rates. The increased demand for labor would lead both to higher wages and to increased employment. Phillips may have seen what he thought he saw.

The late Henry Hazlitt was a noted economist, author, editor, reviewer, and columnist. Best known of his books are *Economics In One Lesson*, *The Failure of the "New Economics*," *The Foundations of Morality*, and *What You Should Know About Inflation*. This article is reprinted from the March 1977 issue of *The Freeman*.

But Keynesian economists, struck by the Phillips thesis, and seeing in it a confirmation of their previous belief, carried it much further. They began to construct Phillips Curves of their own, based not on a comparison of wage rates and employment, but of general prices and employment. And they announced they had found there is a Trade-Off between unemployment and prices. Price stability and reasonably full employment, they asserted, just cannot exist at the same time. The more we get of the one the less we can have of the other. We must make a choice. If we choose a low level of inflation, or none at all, we have to reconcile ourselves to a high level of unemployment. If we choose a low level of unemployment, we must reconcile ourselves to a high rate of inflation.

This alleged dilemma has served as a rationalization for continued inflation in many countries when every other excuse has run out.

The Phillips Curve is a myth, and in the last few years it has been increasingly recognized as a myth. Here is a table comparing the percent changes in the Consumer Price Index, for the 28 years from 1948 to 1975 inclusive, with the percent rate of unemployment in the same years.

Year	Percent Change CPI	Percent Unemployment
1948	7.8	3.8
1949	-1.0	5.9
1950	1.0	5.3
1951	7.9	3.3
1952	2.2	3.0
1953	.8	2.9
1954	.5	5.5
1955	- .4	4.4
1956	1.5	4.1
1957	3.6	4.3
1958	2.7	6.8
1959	.8	5.5
1960	1.6	5.5
1961	1.0	6.7

1962	1.1	5.5
1963	1.2	5.7
1964	1.3	5.2
1965	1.7	4.5
1966	2.9	3.8
1967	2.9	3.8
1968	4.2	3.6
1969	5.4	3.5
1970	5.9	4.9
1971	4.3	5.9
1972	3.3	5.6
1973	6.2	4.9
1974	11.0	5.6
1975	9.1	8.5

Source: Economic Report of the President, January, 1976; pp. 224 and 199.

I leave it to the Phillipists to make what they can of this table. The average annual price rise in the 28 years was 3.2 percent, and the average unemployment rate 4.9 percent. If the alleged Phillips relationship held dependably, then in any year in which the price rise (or "inflation" rate) went above 3.2 percent, the unemployment rate would fall below 4.9 percent. Conversely, in any year in which the "inflation" rate fell below 3.2 percent, the unemployment rate would rise above 4.9 percent. This relationship would hold for all of the 28 years. If, on the other hand, the Phillips Curve were inoperative or nonexistent, the probabilities are that the relationship would hold only about half the time. This is exactly what we find. The Phillips relation occurred in 15 of the 28 years but was falsified in the other 13.

Alternative Views

More detailed analysis of the table hardly helps. An economist who saw what happened only in the years 1948 through 1964 might have been excused for being impressed by the Phillips Curve, for its posited relationship held in 13 of those 17 years. But an economist who saw only what happened in the last 11 of those 28 years—from 1965 through 1975—

might have been equally excused for suspecting that the real relationship was the exact opposite of what the Phillips Curve assumed, for in that period it was borne out in only two years and falsified in nine. And even the economist who seriously studied only what happened in the 1948-1964 period would have noted some strange anomalies. In 1951, when the CPI rose 7.9 percent, unemployment was 3.3 percent; in 1952, when prices rose only 2.2 percent, unemployment fell to 3.0; and in 1953, when prices rose only 8/10 of 1 percent, unemployment *fell* further to 2.9—the lowest for any year on the table.

Phillips statisticians can play with these figures in various ways, to see whether they can extract any more convincing correlation. They can try, for example, to find whether the Phillips relationship held any better if the CPI rise is measured from December to December, or if the calculations are remade to allow for a lag of three months, or six months, or a year, between the "inflation" rate and the unemployment rate. But I do not think they will have any better luck. If the reader will make the count allowing for one year's lag between the price rise and the unemployment figure, for example, he will find the Phillips Curve contention borne out in only 10 and contradicted in the other 18 years.

(I have referred to the rate of the consumer-price rise as the "inflation" rate because that is unfortunately the way the term is applied by the majority of journalists and even economists. Strictly, the term "inflation" should refer only to an increase in the stock of money. A rise of prices is a usual consequence of that increase, though the price rise may be lower or higher than the money increase. Insistence on the distinction between these two terms is not merely pedantic. When the chief consequence of an inflation is itself called the inflation, the real relation of cause and effect is obscured or reversed.)

A clearer picture of the relationship (or nonrelationship) of price rises and unemployment emerges if we take only the last 15 years of the 28 and make our comparisons for the average of five-year periods:

	CPI rise rate (per year)	Unemployment rate (per year)
1961-1965	1.3%	5.5%
1966-1970	4.3%	3.9%
1971-1975	6.8%	6.1%

This table was suggested by one which appeared in Milton Friedman's column in *Newsweek* of December 6, 1976. There are one or two minor changes.

In sum, the highest rate of "inflation" was accompanied by the highest rate of unemployment.

The experience in other nations has been even more striking. In August 1975 The Conference Board published a study comparing the percentages of the work forces *employed* with consumer price indices in seven industrial nations over the preceding fifteen years. By this measurement, in the United States, Canada, and Sweden, the relationship did not noticeably belie the Phillips Curve. (In our 28-year U.S. table, however, we saw that when the price-increase figure shot up in 1974 to 11 percent from a rate of 6.2 percent in 1973, unemployment also rose. If we look at 1975— not shown in the Conference Board study—we find that unemployment soared to 8.5 percent though there was a similar high price rise—9.1 percent—in 1975. Similarly, if we take what happened in 1975 in Canada, we find that though consumer prices rose in that year by the unusually high rate of 10.7 percent, the index of manufacturing employment in Canada *fell* from 108.9 in 1974 to 102.8 in 1975.)

In the four other countries in the Conference Board study, the relationship of employment and inflation was emphatically the opposite of that assumed by the Phillips Curve. The steady price rise in Germany from 1967 to 1973 was accompanied by an equally steady fall in employment. In Japan a rise of 19 percent in consumer prices in 1973 and of 21 percent in 1974 was accompanied by a fall in employment. In Italy, though consumer prices began to soar in 1968, reaching a 25 percent annual rate in 1974, employment declined during the period. In some ways the record of Great Britain, where the Phillips Curve was invented, was the worst of all. Though consumer prices soared 18 percent in 1974 from a rate of 4 percent a decade earlier, employment turned downward. Not shown in the Conference Board compilation was the record of 1975 itself, when the British CPI soared 24 percent—and employment fell further.

But informed economists, with memories, did not need to wait for the experience of the seventies to distrust the relationship posited by the Phillips Curve. In the last and worst months of the great German hyperinflation of 1920-1923, unemployment in the trade unions, which had been 6.3 percent in August, 1923, soared to 9.9 percent in September, 19.1 percent in October, 23.4 percent in November, and 28.2 percent in December.

A Nest of Fallacies

There is a whole nest of fallacies wrapped in the Phillips Curve, and one of them is the implication that the absence of inflation is the sole or at least the chief cause of unemployment. There can be scores of causes for unemployment. One is tempted to say that there can be as many distinguishable causes for unemployment as there are unemployed. But even if we look only at the unemployment brought about by governmental policies, we can find at least a dozen different types of measures that achieve this—minimum-wage laws, laws granting special privileges and immunities to labor unions and imposing special compulsions on employers to make concessions (in the United States, the Norris-LaGuardia Act, Wagner-Taft-Hartley Act, and so forth), unemployment insurance, direct relief, Social Security payments, food stamps, and so on. Whenever unions are given the power to enforce their demands by strike threats and intimidation or by compulsory "collective bargaining" legally imposed on employers, the unions almost invariably extort above-market wage rates that bring about unemployment. Unemployment insurance becomes increasingly generous year by year, and is today paid in some states for as long as 65 weeks. A study prepared for the U.S. Department of Labor in February 1975 finally conceded that "the more liberal the unemployment insurance benefits, the higher the unemployment rate will be."

As long ago as 1934, when the New Deal was being enacted, the economist Benjamin M. Anderson remarked to me in conversation: "We can have just as much unemployment as we want to pay for." The government is today buying a huge amount of it. Yet when the monthly unemployment figures are published, the overwhelming majority of commentators and politicians forget all about this, and attribute the high unemployment figure to insufficient federal spending, insufficient deficits, insufficient inflation.

Another thing wrong with the Phillips Curve is the blind trust its compilers place in the official unemployment statistics. I am not speaking here merely about the amount of guesswork and sampling errors embodied in such statistics, but about the vagueness in the very concept of "full employment." Full employment never means that "everybody has a job" but merely that everybody in the "labor force" has a job. And an immense amount of guesswork goes into estimating the "labor force." Out of a total population estimated in 1975 at 213,631,000, only 92,613,000—or some 43 percent—were estimated as being in the "civilian labor force." These were part of the "noninstitutional" population 16 years of age and over, with certain deductions. As only 84,783,000 persons were estimated as being employed in 1975, this left an average of 7,830,000 "unemployed."

Imprecise Measures

But none of these figures involved exact counts. They were all estimates—subject to various degrees of error. In any case the "unemployed" can never be exactly counted because of the subjective element. As the economist A.C. Pigou put it some forty years ago: "A man is only unemployed when he is *both* not employed and *also* desires to be employed."

It is this second requirement that we can never measure. The U.S. Department of Labor Statistics counts a man as unemployed if he is out of a job and "looking for work." But it is very difficult to determine whether a man is actually looking for a job or how much effort he is making. And when men and women are being paid enough unemployment insurance or relief or food stamps to feel no great urgency to take a job, the raw government statistics can give a very misleading impression of the hardships of all "unemployment."

"Full employment," as bureaucratically defined, is a completely unrealistic goal. It has never been realized in the official figures. Even if there were no governmental policies that created unemployment, it is hardly possible to imagine a situation in which, on the very day any person was laid off, he found a new job with wages and other conditions to his liking. People who give up jobs, and even those who are dropped from them, commonly give themselves an intentional vacation. There is always a certain amount of "frictional," "normal," or "natural" unemployment—averaging in this country, as officially measured, about 5 percent—and government interventions that try persistently to force the figure below this average tend to create inflation and other distortions much worse than the alleged evil they are trying to cure.

To set up "full employment at whatever cost" as the sole or even chief economic goal, results in a distortion and perversion of all values.[3]

The Impact of Inflation

When we put aside all questions of exact quantitative determination and alleged Phillips curves, it is nonetheless clear that inflation does affect employment in numerous ways. It is true that, at its beginning, inflation can tend to create more employment, for the reason that Irving Fisher gave long ago: It tends to increase sales and selling prices faster than it increases costs. But this effect is only temporary, and occurs only to the extent that the inflation is unexpected. For in a short time costs catch up with retail selling prices. To prevent this the inflation must be continued. But as soon as people *expect* the inflation to be continued, they all make compensating adjustments and demands. Unions ask for higher wage rates and "escalating" clauses, lenders demand higher interest rates, including "price premiums," and so on. To keep stimulating employment, it is not enough for the government to continue inflating at the old rate, however high; it must accelerate the inflation. But as soon as people *expect even the acceleration,* this too becomes futile for providing more employment.

Meanwhile, even if the inflation is relatively mild and proceeds at a fairly even rate, it begins to create distortions in the economy. It is amazing how systematically this is overlooked. For most journalists and even most economists make the tacit assumption that an inflation increases prices *uniformly*—that if the wholesale or consumers price index has gone up about 10 percent in the last year, *all* prices have gone up about 10 percent. This assumption is seldom made consciously and *explicitly;* if it were it would be more often detected and refuted.

The assumption is never correct. For (even apart from the wide differences in the elasticity of demand for different commodities) the new money that the government prints and pays out in an inflation does not go proportionately or simultaneously to everybody. It goes, say, to government contractors and their employees, and these first receivers spend it on the particular goods and services they want, The producers of these goods, and their employees, in turn spend the money for still other goods and services. And so on, The first groups spend the money when prices have still gone up least; the final groups when prices have gone up most. In addition, the growing realization that inflation will continue, itself changes the direction of demand—away from thrift and toward luxury spending, for example.

Misallocation and Waste of Scarce Resources

Thus, while inflation is going on it always brings about a misdirection of production and employment. It leads to a condition of temporary demand for various products, a malproduction and a malemployment, a misallocation of resources, that neither can nor should be continued once the inflation is brought to a halt. Thus, at the end of every inflation there is certain to be what is called a "stabilization crisis."

But even the distorted and misdirected employment cannot be indefinitely maintained by continuing or accelerating the inflation. For the inflation, as it goes on, more and more distorts *relative* prices and *relative* wages, and destroys workable relations between particular prices and particular wage rates. While some producers confront swollen and unmeetable demand, others are being driven out of business by wages and other costs rising far faster than their own selling prices. And as inflation accelerates it becomes impossible for individual producers to make any dependable estimate of the wage rates and other costs they will have to meet in the next few months, or their own future selling prices, or the margin between the two. The result is not only increasing malemployment but increasing *un*employment. This was tragically illustrated, for example, in the last months of the German hyperinflation.

Nor can the government mitigate the situation by any such further intervention as "indexing." If it tries to insure, for example, that all workers are paid the average increase that has occurred in wages or prices, it will not only increase wages over the previous average but put out of business even sooner the producers who have not been able, because of lack of demand, to raise their selling prices as much as the average. Every attempt to correct previous distortions and inequities by government ukase will only create worse distortions and inequities. There is no cure but to halt the inflation. This is itself an operation not without its cost; but that cost is infinitely less than that of continuing the inflation—or even of trying to slow it down "gradually."

In sum, an inflation can increase employment only temporarily, only to the extent that it is unexpected, and only when it is comparatively mild and in its early stages. Its long-run effect is to misdirect employment and finally to destroy it. The belief that inflation increases employment is perhaps the most costly myth of the present age.

---

1. "A Statistical Relation between Unemployment and Price Changes," *International Labor Review*, June 1926, pp. 785-792. Milton Friedman has recently called attention to the article.

2. "The Relation between Unemployment and the Rate of Change of Money Wage Rates in the United Kingdom, 1861-1957," *Economica*, November, 1958, pp. 283-299.

3. The present writer has discussed this question more fully in Ch. XXVI: "'Full Employment' as the Goal," *The Failure of the "New Economics,"* 1959.

Lower Interest Rates by Law

by Percy L. Greaves, Jr.

Why would it be a mistake for Federal Reserve officials to lower interest rates?

Wouldn't it help the building industry? It would seem that a reduction in interest rates would lead to a renewal of building activity. This would put a lot of people to work and provide a lot more homes for those who want them. In fact, wouldn't lower interest rates be a spur to other industries and be good for the country as a whole?

The answer is easy. If lower interest rates were *free market* interest rates, business would boom and bid up wage rates. However, if lower interest rates were the result of a government fiat, the effects would be disastrous. As the late Professor Ludwig von Mises frequently stated, every political interference with free market processes makes matters worse, not better, even from the viewpoint of those who propose such political interferences.

The reason for this is often difficult to understand. Unfortunately, those who attempt to push down interest rates by legal edict do not foresee the inevitable undesirable consequences. In recent years many people have learned the hard way about the consequences of political price and wage controls. Learning from experience the consequences of political interest-rate controls could be even more painful.

When the government attempts to maintain prices *above* those of the free and unhampered market, as it has with some farm products, this inevitably leads to surpluses. Too much land, labor, and scarce materials are devoted to producing such subsidized goods. This has two results. First, there are surpluses which must be stored, destroyed, or given away. Second, the land, labor, and scarce materials are not available to produce those goods and services which consumers desire in larger quantities. We know this because there are people willing to pay more than the free mar-

---

The late Professor Greaves was a free-lance economist and lecturer. His books included *Understanding the Dollar Crisis* and *Mises Made Easier* (Glossary for *Human Action*). This article appeared in the December 1974 issue of *The Freeman*.

ket production costs of such goods and yet cannot find them on the market.

When the government attempts to maintain prices *below* those that would prevail in a free and unhampered market, as it recently did with price controls, this inevitably leads to shortages such as we experienced in a matter of months. In addition to the shortages, we soon had more unemployed workers, factories, and transportation facilities, not to mention the increased welfare expenses this made necessary.[1] Businessmen, being human, will not continue to produce what they cannot sell at prices that cover their costs. Their available capital will not long permit it.

When the government attempts to raise wage rates above those that would prevail in a free and unhampered market, as it has for some forty years, it inevitably produces unemployment or *under*employment with an accompanying demand for welfare payments. Such welfare payments are a burden on all who buy goods and services in the marketplace. The unemployment and *under*employment mean higher prices because fewer goods and services are produced to compete for the consumers' limited number of dollars.

When the government grants privileges to labor unions to raise wage rates above those of a free and competitive market, it raises the costs of producing union-made goods and services. The resulting higher prices inevitably reduce sales. This in turn reduces employment in such industries, or in other industries whose sales fall off because consumers, paying higher prices for union-made goods and services, have less for other things. This means that those who could have worked in the curtailed industries must look elsewhere for jobs and accept lower wages or remain unemployed and eventually increase the need for welfare payments. Those who take jobs at lower wage rates than they could have had in a free market will be *under*employed. That is, they will be producing goods or services less desired by consumers than those that have been priced out of the market by the legal privileges which permit labor unions to extort higher than free market wages from society.

Such ill-fated attempts to raise wage rates above those earned in a free market inevitably force more and more unfortunate workers to take lower-paying jobs. Eventually, with the growth of labor union power, the competition for such lower-paying jobs drives some wages so low that many workers find it difficult to maintain their previous standard of living. Those who believe that political power can raise *all* wage rates then advocate minimum wage laws. Such laws compel employers to pay all their employees at least the minimum wage. Employers, being human and having limited resources, soon refuse to employ those for whom the minimum wage rate raises production costs above what customers will pay. Such unfortunate persons, including many youngsters, members of minority races and others with limited skills, then become legally unemployable. Their bleak choice is between a life of crime or subsistence on welfare payments until the value of the dollar is reduced by inflation to the point where they become employable at the legal minimum wage rate.

There was no long-term mass unemployment in this country when everyone was free to take the highest wage rate that any employer could and would offer for his or her services. Market competition forced employers to pay their workers the full market value of their contribution. If they failed to do so, other employers would bid away such underpaid workers. Political interferences in the labor market, with the intentions of raising *all* wage rates, have created our present mass unemployment, *under*employment, and the growing need for welfare payments. Only a return to a free and unhampered labor market will bring to an end such unemployment and *under*employment. In a free market there are jobs for all[2] and no need to subsidize in idleness those who are able to work.

The Market Produces Interest Rates

Interest rates, like prices and wage rates, are market phenomena. Political interferences with interest rates, like price and wage controls, create economic chaos. Such chaos leads to a general loss of freedom and inevitably reduces the living standards of every member of society. It is thus vital that we all understand why the government should not interfere with free market interest rates.

Market interest rates are a sum of three contributing market factors.

(1) The first is true or pure interest; what Mises called "originary interest." This is payment for time preference. A person currently short of cash may wish to spend $1,000 for something now, and pay for it later when he expects to have more cash. If he wants that object so badly *now* that he is willing to promise to pay $1,100 a year from now, he may be able to obtain an immediate loan of $1,000. That would mean he values spending the $1,000 now so much more than waiting a year to do so that

he is willing to pay 10 percent, or $100, more to have the object now.

In order to borrow this $1,000, the borrower must find someone who has saved $1,000 and is willing to lend it to him for one year for an interest rate of 10 percent or less. Few people will lend their savings, except for charitable purposes, without receiving some benefit in return. The prospective lender may want to buy a car or take a trip at the end of a year. He will make the loan only on condition that he be repaid an extra sum for making the sacrifice of not spending his money now. That extra payment, called interest, must be high enough for the prospective lender to value the future repayment, with interest, higher than he values spending the $1,000 now. So the loan depends on each party's placing a higher value on what he receives than on what he furnishes the other party. The difference between the sum loaned and the sum to be repaid is true or pure interest—a payment that will compensate a saver for postponing his own spending for the time of the loan.

(2) The second factor in market interest rates is the certainty or un-certainty that the loan will be repaid as specified. If there is valuable collateral or if the lender thinks the chances of repayment are good, this factor will be minimal. However, if the borrower has few resources and there is reason to believe that the loan might not be repaid if he died or lost his job, this would be a factor the lender would consider in arriving at the total interest rate he would request before making a loan to that specific person. This factor would differ from person to person and from loan to loan, but it is present to some extent in the interest rate on every loan.

(3) The third and currently most important factor in market interest rates is what is expected to happen to the purchasing power of the dollar during the term of the loan. If the lender expects prices to rise 10 percent in the next year and he only gets 10 percent more dollars back from the borrower at the end of the year, he does not receive one cent of pure interest. Pure interest is only the amount the lender gets back over and above the purchasing power he has lent. So in times of inflation, when the value of the dollar is going down, this third factor must rise. As it rises, so does the market interest rate, which is the total of the three factors just discussed—(1) pure interest based on time preference, (2) uncertainty of repayment, and (3) change in the dollar's purchasing power.

Current market interest rates are considered high because this third factor, reflecting an anticipated drop in the dollar's purchasing power, is high. The way to reduce this factor is to reduce the expectation that the purchasing power of the dollar will drop in the next year. So the only satisfactory way to reduce current high interest rates is to eliminate the expectation that future prices will be ever higher. This means we must stop the inflation.

More Savings Are Needed

Lower interest rates that represent free market interest rates are always helpful to society in general. Lower interest rates in a free market society mean there are comparatively more savers with funds they want to lend than there are borrowers who will pay high interest rates. These savers seek to lend their funds so as to earn as much money as possible. Rather than spend their savings now, they seek more funds at a later date when their current income may be lower, as when they retire, or when their expenses may be higher, as when they may want to buy a car or a house or send a child to college. It is the higher amounts of such savings, bidding in the marketplace for borrowers, that produce lower interest rates in a free society. To bring about such lower interest rates, government should protect and encourage voluntary loans made with the expectation they will be repaid in dollars with the same or an increasing purchasing power.

But the question in many minds today is, why not have the Federal Reserve System lower market interest rates by fiat? The answer is simply this: If the Federal Reserve lowers interest rates when there are no increased savings available for lending, there will be a bigger demand for loans at the lower interest rate than can be made with available savings. Under present laws and conditions, the banks meet this increased demand for loans at the lower interest rates by creating more loan money out of thin air (or should we say paper?). The borrowers get their loans in the form of an addition to their bank accounts on which they can draw checks. No one else has chosen to reduce his spending so as to make his savings available to the borrower, as is always the case with free market credit transactions.

Why Interest Rate Controls Hurt

When the Federal Reserve System reduces interest rates by fiat, it must create more spendable money than was previously earned or saved. It puts into the market dollars which do not represent any contribution to society. You have more dollars in the hands of borrowers and no reduction in the numbers of dollars which savers may spend currently. This has several undesirable effects, some obvious and others largely unseen.

The most obvious effect is that with more money bidding for the same quantity of goods and services in the marketplace, prices must be higher than they would otherwise be. Largely unseen are the ways in which this increased quantity of money enters the marketplace and how it affects the structure of production and the welfare of different individuals.

Those who borrow the savings of people who must reduce their current expenditures and those who borrow artificially created bank money cannot be distinguished in the marketplace. In fact, most borrowers from banks do not know whether they are borrowing the funds of the bank's stockholders and depositors or newly created funds. The borrowers of the newly created funds are in a position to bid away available goods from the earners and savers who would have bought them if the quantity of dollars had not been increased. What such borrowers buy drives prices up and leaves less for all who earned or saved the money they take to market. In the short run, these artificially lower interest rates help borrowers and those who sell to them—the construction industry if the borrowers buy houses—at the expense of all workers, savers, and those who would have profited from supplying what the workers and savers can no longer buy.

Outstanding Contracts Affected

Although some may be helped by such artificial lowering of interest rates, all who have earned or saved money are hurt. Such creation of more dollars not only hurts all workers and savers, by reducing the value of their dollars, but it also affects the value of every outstanding contract. It means every pre-existing dollar is worth less and every contract promising to pay dollars in the future has been altered in favor of the payer and to the disadvantage of the recipient. This means a reduction in the real value of all bank accounts, insurance policies, wage rates, salaries, and pensions as well as all rental contracts, time payments and other purchase agreements. When savers foresee such effects, they refuse to make any more loans unless the interest rates will more than compensate them for the expected drop in the value of the dollars they lend.

The most important, generally unrealized, effect of such artificial increases in the quantity of spendable dollars is that they redirect the whole economy. They do so in a manner that cannot be continued without an ever-increasing quantity of newly created dollars to compensate for the resulting higher prices. As the political increase in the quantity of dollars accelerates, more and more of the nation's production facilities are devoted to supplying the spenders of the newly created dollars. This means a smaller and smaller part of the production facilities are devoted to supplying the nation's workers and savers. Eventually, if the process is not stopped in time, the system breaks down and the dollars become worthless.

Stopping Inflation Has a Price

Of course, the process can be stopped at any time, but not without consequences. Once the government stops increasing the quantity of dollars artificially or even slows down the rate of artificial increase in the quantity of dollars, producers supplying goods and services to the spenders of newly created unearned dollars lose a large number of their customers. They must then lay off men and there is a recession or depression—until production is adjusted to supplying only those with earned or saved dollars to spend.

Under present policies the government is continually faced with deciding whether to inflate artificially the quantity of spendable dollars or permit market forces to readjust the economy. If free and unhampered market forces are permitted to emerge, free market prices, wage rates, and interest rates will quickly redirect the economy toward a more efficient satisfaction of all those who contribute toward production. Those who had spent newly created dollars will have to curb their spending or earn the dollars they spend. The available supplies of workers and capital goods will be quickly redirected toward producing solely for those spending dollars they have earned or saved in the service of their fellowmen.

In short, when Federal Reserve officials lower interest rates artificially, they send a part of the economy off on a spree at the expense of the nation's workers and savers. The spree can only be continued by an ever-increasing inflation of the quantity of spendable dollars. If we want to end that inflation and all its undesirable consequences, we must permit the free market to determine interest rates as borrowers compete for the real savings made available by those willing to reduce their potential spending temporarily for a price, commonly called interest. Only freely determined interest rates, without any artificial manipulation or control of the quantity of dollars, will eliminate the inflation problem from our economy.

The best way to reduce market interest rates is to remove the expectancy of further inflation. Once this is done, more people will be encouraged to save more dollars and their competition for borrowers will bring lower market interest rates. Then there can be a profitable expansion of those industries that will direct available supplies of labor and capital into producing more of the things that workers and savers want most.

The only way Federal Reserve officials can help workers, investors, and consumers is to stop increasing the quantity of dollars—stop inflating—and permit free market forces to set interest rates that reflect the actual supply of, and demand for, such savings as are available for lending. Any interference with free market interest rates must upset the economy and produce results that all honest and intelligent people consider undesirable.

---

1. People who sanction laws which deprive some workers from earning a living for themselves and their families are honor bound to provide the necessities of life for such second-class citizens.

2. See author's "Jobs for All," *The Freeman,* February 1959.

Demand Deposit Inflation

by Anthony M. Reinach

Suppose that yours is a small community which, before automobiles, would have been referred to as a "one-horse" town. Today it might be called a "one-gasoline-station" town. Its government is centered in a mayor who has promised to render generous services on a parsimonious budget. Actually, the mayor seems to be achieving his contradictory objectives. In truth, however, he has prevailed upon the proprietor of the town's only gasoline station to mix his gas with water and share with the town government the profits generated by the dilution. The exposure of this knavery triggers a campaign to justify it as "government policy in the interest of the people." Notwithstanding, I suspect that righteous indignation will still be aroused in even the town's most benign citizens.

Although such knavery is, of course, ludicrous, it is just as ludicrous that citizens, in respect to their money, passively permit their Federal government to victimize them by essentially the same fraud as described above. The fact that this fraud, monetary inflation, will uncontestably perpetrate more injustice in the next decade than did the Spanish Inquisition at its height suggests that there are precious few individuals who really understand monetary inflation.

Technologically, money has taken three basic forms: commodity, paper, and checking account funds. Collaterally, monetary inflation has evolved from coin debasement, to printing press, to the creation of spurious demand deposits. Because demand deposits are the monetary tools employed in over 90 percent of America's financial transactions, it is demand inflation that is destined to make history's most notorious swindles look like Tootsie Roll thefts by comparison.

Mr. Reinach, a New York businessman, free-lance writer, and monetary economist, wrote this article for the January 1968 issue of *The Freeman*.

Recipe for Inflation

To understand how demand deposit inflation works, imagine yourself in the role of a drugstore owner. The name of your drugstore is Fiscal Pharmacy, and you operate it with one employee, Samuel. You wish to remodel your store at a cost of $10,000, but all your funds are being used for other purposes and you have already stretched your credit to just the last penny. It seems that you will have to abandon, or at least postpone, your remodeling program. But then you get an idea!

You go to your local printer and instruct him to print up $10,000 worth of 30-year bonds on Fiscal Pharmacy, to yield 3½ percent. In addition, you instruct your printer to make up a checkbook for "The Samuel Trust Company." A few days later, armed with the freshly printed bonds and checkbook, you summon Samuel to inform him of a proprietary position with which you are about to reward him for his loyalty:

> *You*: I have decided to remodel Fiscal Pharmacy. It will take $10,000.
> *Samuel*: That's a lot of potatoes.
> *You*: Yes, and I haven't been able to raise the first dollar.
> *Samuel*: Maybe you should cut your personal living expenses.
> *You*: And have my wife throw me out?
> *Samuel*: So what do you propose?
> *You*: Here's my plan. From now on, you will function not only as a clerk, but also as the private banker for Fiscal Pharmacy.
> *Samuel*: But I haven't got $10,000.
> *You*: You won't need it. In fact, you won't need any of it.
> *Samuel*: No?
> *You*: No. Here's $10,000 worth of bonds on Fiscal Pharmacy and a checkbook for "The Samuel Trust Company." Your bank now owns the bonds, so please pay for them by issuing a $10,000 check to Fiscal Pharmacy.

Having deposited this check with a conventional bank—conventional, that is, except for its naivete you now have the wherewithal for your remodeling program.

The funds you subsequently transfer to your contractor will soon be transferred by him to his own creditors and others, and so forth. Thus begins the process by which the $10,000 you and Samuel conspired to create become diffused throughout America's entire commercial banking system. However, the atomized dispersion of that $10,000 will in no way diminish its impact on the nation's money supply.

Because banks are permitted by law to lend out roughly 80 percent of their deposits, and because banks, since World War II, have been vigorously lending out virtually every dollar allowed by law, an additional $8,000 (80 percent of $10,000) of loans or investments in credit instruments, which is the same thing—will be promptly made.

These new loans will be promptly returned to the banking system as new demand deposits and will, in turn, enable the banks to lend out another $6,400 (80 percent of $8,000), which will likewise be deposited and generate the additional lending of $5,120, et cetera, et cetera, et cetera. The result will be $40,000 of derivative demand deposits spawned from the initial bogus $10,000 demand deposit, for a grand total of $50,000.

The Government Procedure that Triggers Inflation

Fictitious? Yes. Fantastic? No. With one major modification, the conspiratorial procedure by which you and Samuel created the initial bogus $10,000 is essentially the same procedure by which government triggers monetary inflation. How such money mushrooms into five times its original amount is not even privileged information; indeed, it is publicized by the government itself.

Monetary inflation begins with the Federal budget which, let us suppose, is $150 billion. To raise this money, the government can tax, borrow, or inflate. Let us further suppose that the government taxes $100 billion and borrows $40 billion, still leaving it $10 billion short. At this point, were my drugstore analogy procedurally accurate, the U. S. Treasury would enter in the role of Fiscal Pharmacy's owner, and the Federal Reserve would enter in the role of Samuel, Fiscal Pharmacy's private banker:

> *Treasury:* Our expenses this year are $150 billion.
> *Fed:* That's a lot of potatoes.
> *Treasury:* We were able to tax only $100 billion.
> *Fed:* Maybe you should raise taxes by 50 percent.
> *Treasury:* And get voted out of office?

Fed: Well, how much were you able to borrow?
Treasury: $40 billion.
Fed: That still leaves you $10 billion short.
Treasury: Yes, so here's $10 billion worth of bonds. Please issue a check in payment for them.

If the actual procedure were this brazen, the naked chicanery of monetary inflation would be too fully exposed. Consequently, the Treasury rarely sells government bonds directly to the Fed. Instead, the Treasury simply notifies the Fed when it has unsold bonds. The Fed, in turn, starts buying government bonds in the open market with the exclusive purpose of creating the very marketplace climate required by the Treasury to liquidate its sticky inventory. The final result, of course, is the same as if the Treasury had sold the bonds directly to the Fed in the first place. In fact, the net result may be even more inflationary; it is quite possible that the Fed might have to buy $11 billion worth of bonds in the market to enable the Treasury to dispose of $10 billion.

The Fed claims to have three weapons of direct control over monetary inflation. But this claim would be valid only under circumstances which would make the weapons unnecessary: (a) when the government is balancing its budget, or (b) when the government, having failed to balance its budget, is willing to sell its bonds on a free market basis. When neither situation prevails, the Fed's alleged weapons are rendered impotent and simply serve as disguises for monetary inflation. Those three weapons are:

1. Open Market Operations
2. Reserve Requirements
3. Discount Rate (or Rediscount Rate)

Open Market Operations

Open market operations are simply the buying and selling of government bonds by the Fed. One side of the open market operation coin has already been demonstrated—the buying of government bonds to help the Treasury sell its own. In theory, after the Treasury is rid of its bonds, the Fed turns around and starts merchandizing its own recent purchases. In practice, regrettably, the Treasury is rarely without bonds for sale, at least these days. As a result, the Fed's ownership of government bonds has increased from $26 billion to $48 billion on the past seven years, and *that* is the launching pad destined to rocket prices in the forthcoming decade.

Reserve Requirements Tend Toward Zero

As already stated, banks are permitted by law to lend out roughly 80 percent of their deposits. The figure today is nearer 85 percent but 80 percent illustrates the point and is easy to figure. The difference between 80 percent and 100—20 percent—is, correspondingly, the figure commonly used as the average reserve requirement for the three categories of commercial banks which are members of the Federal Reserve System. This means that these member banks must deposit with the Fed 20 percent of their total demand deposits. By raising reserve requirements, the Fed would deter part or all the inflationary impact threatened by its government bond purchases. This, however, would "tighten money," which would cause higher interest rates, and would thereby make it more difficult for the subsequent sales of government bonds at "favorable" rates of interest. As a result, reserve requirements for city banks have not been raised in over 15 years. (On November 24, 1960, the reserve requirement for country banks was raised from 11 to 12 percent.)

The discount rate is the interest rate member banks must pay the Fed for borrowing money from it. When a bank becomes temporarily "under-reserved" (has more than 80 percent of its demand deposits out on loan, which is the same as having less than 20 percent of its demand deposits available for deposit with the Fed), it has a choice of either borrowing from the Fed or liquidating some of its loans. In theory, the second course of action will counter inflation whereas borrowing from the Fed will not. Therefore, to carry the theory further, raising the discount rate will discourage borrowing and thereby counter inflation, and lowering the discount rate will encourage borrowing and thereby stimulate inflation. Ironically, this theory more often than not operates in reverse. Prompted by a costly discount rate to counter inflation through the liquidation of loans, commercial banks usually begin by selling some of *their* government bonds. This, in turn, will cause consternation in U.S. Treasury circles, which will instigate telephone calls to the Fed, which will trigger open market purchases, which will add more fuel to the inflationary fire than was initially withdrawn by raising the discount rate. For this reason, the discount rate is useless as a weapon to combat inflation.

Prime Commercial Paper is America's most valued interest-bearing credit instrument, and its interest rates are the most sensitive to shifts in financial sentiment. Since World War I, there have been 24 trend reversals in the Federal Reserve discount rate. Without exception, these trend reversals were preceded by trend reversals in Commercial Paper interest rates. In other words, and notwithstanding the lofty pronouncements of "positive constructive action" that attended many of these 24 trend reversals, the Federal Reserve discount rate for half a century has been tagging after the Prime Commercial Paper rate like an obedient puppy.

Change in Discount Rate a Powerless Weapon

Twice, in 1926 and again in 1927, when stock market speculation rather than monetary inflation was the object of "summit" control, the Fed reversed the discount rate trend by reducing it half a percentage point. In total disregard of prior reductions in Commercial Paper rates, an entire generation of monetary intellectuals has been placing part of the blame for the subsequent stock market boom and bust on one or both of those two discount rate reductions. Even the Fed's own documents make it abundantly evident that the discount rate is just as powerless to combat the current generation's inflation as it was to combat the last generation's stock market boom.

Over the years, the Fed also has enlisted gold to minify the threat of inflation. Until the early 1960s: "Gold [was] the basis of Reserve Bank credit because . . . the power of the Reserve Banks to create money through adding to their deposits or issuing Federal Reserve notes is limited by the requirement of a 25 percent reserve in gold certificates against both kinds of liabilities. That is to say, the total of Federal Reserve notes and deposits must not exceed four times the amount of gold certificates held by the Reserve Banks. Thus, the ultimate limit on Federal Reserve credit expansion is set by gold." Yet, on the preceding page in the same publication, the Fed confesses that when circumstances in 1945 "threatened to impinge upon the Federal Reserve's freedom of policy action . . . . , Congress deemed it wise to reduce the reserve requirement of the Reserve Banks from 40 percent for Federal Reserve notes and 35 percent for deposits to 25 percent for each kind of liability."[1]

In 1963, Dean Russell concluded: "Whenever the technical cutoff relationship between gold and 'money' has been approached in the past, Congress has modified it—and will unquestionably do so in the future, even to the point of abolishing the technical requirement altogether."[2] Was Dean being a prophet, or just a realist?

Or perhaps Dean was simply taking the Fed at its word for, by 1963, it was no longer terming "gold ... the basis of Reserve Bank credit . . .", but was saying instead: ". . . reserves in gold constitute a statutory base for Reserve Bank power to create Federal Reserve credit." Then, two years later, came the dismantling of that "statutory base": "The law determining the minimum holdings of gold certificates required as reserves against the Federal Reserve Banks' liabilities was changed on March 3, 1965. The Reserve Banks are no longer required to hold 25 percent reserves against their deposit liabilities, but they are still required to hold gold certificates equal to at least 25 percent of their note liabilities." Was Dean's predicted reason correct, that "the technical cutoff relationship between gold and 'money' (was being) approached"? Letting the Fed speak for itself: "If the change had not been made, the amount of 'free' gold certificates on March 31, 1965, would have been [down to] $1.0 billion."[3]

Monetary and Other Factors Affect Impact of Inflation

There are many minor monetary factors constantly influencing the impact of inflation. One of the more important is the conversion of demand deposits into cash, and vice versa. For example, the withdrawal of $100 from your checking account not only immediately reduces demand deposits by $100, but also ultimately extinguishes an additional $400 of derivative demand deposits. Consequently, money is customarily "tight" just before Christmas—when the demand for cash is at its height.

There are also many "non-monetary" factors constantly influencing the impact of inflation. The standard here is productivity. Thus, the most aggravating factor is war, and the most moderating factors are technological advances and industrial expansion. Labor strikes, because they curb production, aggravate the impact of inflation. Labor contracts that result in the curtailment of labor-saving devices also aggravate the impact of inflation, but labor contracts that merely call for the escalation of wages do not. A population increase of productive citizens moderates inflation's impact, but a population increase of nonproductive citizens or a popu-

146 / Anthony M. Reinach

lation decrease of productive citizens aggravates it. England's "brain drain" must aggravate the impact of that nation's inflation, but will moderate the impact of America's inflation to the extent that we inherit those "brains." The flight of capital to foreign countries is an aggravating factor whereas the influx of foreign capital is a moderating factor. In a related vein, a so-called "favorable balance of trade" is an aggravating factor whereas an "unfavorable balance of trade" has a moderating effect.

Assessing the Consequences

Some factors which seem to counter the impact of inflation actually intensify it, and vice versa. For example, credit and price controls, inflation's two most inevitable corollaries after rising prices, put sand in the gears of production. Both, thereby, intensify the impact of inflation. On the other hand, increases in the velocity of money (its change-of-hands frequency) are inflationary in theory, but, in reality, counter the impact of inflation. The reason is that most money velocity increases are attended by and generate even greater production increases.

Far more crucial than the factors influencing the impact of inflation are and will be its withering consequences on American life. Historically, every nation whose government resorted to monetary inflation suffered unremitting demotions of its "general welfare." Nor has any government ever abandoned an entrenched policy of monetary inflation. Therefore, barring the revocation of the lessons of history, one need not be a prophet to chart America's economic future.

For 2,500 years, man has been given but two grim choices in respect to his money: "managed" and "convertible gold standard." Chronic monetary inflation goes with a "managed" money system just as chronic money panics go with a "convertible gold standard" money system. The 19 or more money panics that afflicted America in her 170 "convertible gold standard" years negate "convertible gold standard" money as a rational alternative to "managed" money. The only remaining alternative is free enterprise money. This, of course, would require the elimination of government from the money business.

---

1. *The Federal Reserve System, Purposes and Functions,* 3rd edition, sixth printing, 1959, pp. 96 and 97.

2. Dean Russell, "Money, Banking, Debt and Inflation," unpublished paper, 1963.

3. *The Federal Reserve System, Purposes and Functions*, 5th edition, 1st printing, 1963; 2nd printing, 1965; pp. 165 and 175.

The Making of an International Monetary Crisis

by Paul Stevens

For years the world has been plagued by continuing international monetary crises. The international monetary system since 1944 has endured dollar shortages and dollar gluts; chronic deficits and chronic surpluses; perpetual parity disequilibria and currency realignments; disruptive "hot money" flights of capital, and numerous controls on the exchange of money and goods.

In 1968 a "two-tier" gold market was established in the midst of a run on U. S. Treasury gold reserves. In 1971 the two-tier experiment failed in the face of new foreign government demands for dollar convertibility: the United States embargoed gold and allowed the dollar to seek its own level on the free market.

In December of 1971, a new agreement was reached—the Smithsonian Agreement—which consisted of multilateral revaluations of most major foreign currencies and a *de facto* devaluation of the dollar. In 1972 the dollar was officially devalued yet remained nonconvertible into gold.

Further Devaluation

Meanwhile, only fourteen months after the Smithsonian Agreement was reached, the dollar was brought under new selling pressure and was again forced to devalue (a total of almost 20 percent in under two years), and the free market price of gold soared to nearly $100 an ounce, making the official price and the now mythical "two-tier" system look embarrassingly unrealistic.

The most immediate and visible cause of the 1971 international monetary crisis can be traced directly to an excess supply of dollars which have been accumulating in foreign central banks. These dollars, some $60 billion, were at one time theoretically claims on U. S. gold. But over the

Mr. Stevens, a free-lance writer specializing in the field of economics, wrote this article for the April 1973 issue of *The Freeman*.

years, U. S. gold reserves (now about $10 billion) have become conspicuously inadequate to meet foreign demand for gold convertibility.

At present, the major problem confronting economic and monetary Policy Makers is: "What is to be done with the approximately $60 billion held by the central banks of the Western world?"

Policy Makers have instituted one stop-gap measure after another in order to buy the time necessary to solve this problem and to reach agreement on long-term monetary reform. Agreement on monetary reform will be the basis for the development of a new international monetary system, tentatively scheduled to be established by the International Monetary Fund (IMF) in the near future.

But before one can determine which reforms are necessary for a successful future monetary system, one must know what monetary policies caused the past system to fail.

Today's Policy Makers have refused to identify the most fundamental cause of the 1971 international monetary crisis; they have never wanted to know which monetary theories and policies led to the excessive and disruptive amounts of dollars that now flood the world, for the answer is: their own monetary theories and domestic policies of artificial money and credit expansion. If one wishes to project the kinds of policies that will be employed internationally and the effects they will produce in the future, one need only to look at the monetary theories held by today's Policy Makers and their effects when implemented in the past.

Monetary Theory: Past

During the nineteenth century the free world was on what was called the classical gold standard. It was a century of unprecedented production. More wealth and a greater standard of living was achieved and enjoyed by more people than in all of the previous history of the world. The two conditions most responsible for the great increase in wealth during the nineteenth century were competitive capitalism and the gold standard: Capitalism because it provided a social system where men were free to *produce* and *own* the results of their labor; the gold standard because it provided a monetary system by which men could more readily *exchange* and *save* the results of their labor.

While capitalism afforded men the opportunity to trade in the open market which led to economic *prosperity,* the gold standard provided a market-originated medium of exchange and means of saving which led to monetary *stability*.

But because neither competitive capitalism nor the gold standard was ever fully understood or practiced, there existed a paradox during the nineteenth century: a series of disruptive economic and monetary crises in the midst of a century of prosperity.

These crises can all be traced to excessive supplies of money and credit. The U.S. panics of 1814, 1819, 1837, 1857, 1873, 1893, 1907, and the international monetary crises of 1933 and 1971 all have one thing in common: excessive supplies of money and credit. The fact is that no monetary crisis in history has ever resulted from a *lack* of money and credit. *Every* monetary crisis can be traced to excessive supplies of money and credit. Where does this money and credit come from?

Under a gold standard, the amount of money in circulation is the amount of gold circulating among individuals or held in trust by banks. All claims to gold (e.g., dollars) are receipts for gold and are fully convertible into a specific amount of gold. If the claims to gold are circulating, the gold cannot. The money supply is determined in the open market—by the same factors that determine the production of any and all commodities—the factors of supply, demand, and the costs of production. Thus the only way to increase wealth under such a market-originated monetary and economic system is through the production of goods or services.

No Curb on Governments

But the world never achieved a pure gold standard. While individuals operated under a classical gold standard with the conviction that production was the only way to gain wealth, they allowed their government to become the exception to this rule.

Government produces nothing. During the nineteenth century it operated mostly on money it taxed from its citizens. As government's role increased, so did its need for money.

The Policy Makers knew that gold stood in the way of government spending, that direct confiscation of wealth via taxation was unpopular. So Policy Makers advocated a way of indirectly taxing productive men in order to finance both government programs and the increasing government bureaucracy necessary to implement those programs.

The method was to increase the money supply. Since government officials were not about to go out and mine gold, they had to rely on an artificial increase. Although the methods of artificial monetary expansion varied, the net effect remained the same: an increase in the claims to goods in circulation and a general rise in commodity prices. The layman called this phenomenon "inflation." This resulted invariably in monetary crises and economic depressions.

Capitalism and gold got the blame for these crises, but the blame was undeserved.

Why then were capitalism and the gold standard not exonerated from this unearned guilt? Why were these two great institutions tried and sentenced to death by the slow strangulation of government laws? The verdict must read: "Found guilty due to inadequate defense."

The few whispers of defense from a handful of scholars were easily drowned out by every politician who argued for more government controls and regulations over the economy; by every professor who argued for the redistribution of private wealth and for government to provide for the welfare of some group at the expense of another; by every businessman and his lobbyist who argued for government to subsidize his business or industry while protecting him from foreign competitors; by every economist who advocated that government should "stimulate" the economy; and by every media spokesman who argued that the public should vote for policies of government intervention. These, and men like them, made up an army of educators.

The Policy Makers

They were the "intellectuals" who promoted theories that could not exist without the governmental expropriation of private funds; who sponsored, advocated, or encouraged government policies that would victimize men (taxation), deceive and defraud men (inflation), and turn men against one another (the redistribution of private wealth). They were the men who provided government with the theoretical ammunition necessary to disarm men of their rights. They educated the public on the "blessings" of government intervention, and were the ones directly or indirectly responsible for all the subsequent coercive government actions and all of their economically disruptive effects.

They were (and still are) the Policy Makers.

Policy Makers damned capitalism and the gold standard as being inherently unstable. They attributed capitalism's productive booms to government's intervention into the economy, and the government-made busts to the gold standard and the "greed of man."

Such distortions of truth could not be sold to the public easily. A united attack on common sense was necessary in order to obscure the virtues of freedom and the meaning of money.

The Process of Confusion

The Policy Maker led that attack. Armed with the slogans of a con man, he slowly obscured the obvious and concealed the sensible, cloaking monetary and economic theories in graphs, charts, and statistics, until men doubted their own ability to deal with the now esoteric problems of economy and state.

But the American public had great confidence in the integrity of their public leaders and trusted the knowledge of experts in the fields of higher learning, and so they accepted the conclusions of their Policy Makers.

The Policy Maker had made his first and most important move toward institutionalizing government intervention and his theories of artificial monetary expansion into the American way of life: he convinced the American public that men needed government protection from the "natural" depressions of capitalism and the monetary crises "inherent" in the gold standard.

Policy Makers had to do a lot of talking to convince men that the most productive system ever known to them was the cause of depressions. They had to do even more talking to convince men that the precious metal freely chosen and held as money was the cause of monetary depreciation and the source of bank insolvency. It took a lot of talking, but when they had finished, men were convinced. They were convinced that their minds—their own eyes—had been deceiving them. They were convinced that the way to freedom was through greater controls and more restrictions, and that paper was as good as gold.

While the attack on capitalism was subtle and implicit, condemnation of the gold standard was open and explicit.

Condemnation of Gold

The reason for the Policy Maker's condemnation is that, even though governments never really adhered to it, the gold standard placed limits on the amount of artificial money and credit a government could create. Money and credit expansion was always brought to a quick end because banks and governments had to redeem their notes in gold. Redemption was the major obstacle in the way of the Policy Maker's dream of unlimited artificial money creation, unlimited spending.

The Policy Maker learned how to obtain in a matter of minutes the purchasing power of 50 productive men working 50 weeks. He learned of the plunder and loot that a button on a printing press would provide. But it would not be until the twentieth century that he would convince the government to eliminate gold and convince men of the "virtues" of legal counterfeiting. The Policy Maker had to destroy man's idea of property in order to entice men with dreams of unearned wealth. He had to persuade men of the "merits" of monetary redistribution and government handouts.

If there was a monetary rule of conduct among men during the days of the semi-gold standard it was: the man who desires to gain wealth must earn it, by producing goods or their equivalent in gold.

It was in this spirit and by this *golden* rule of conduct that men could and did operate in the monetary and economic spheres of society. Consequently, they achieved the most productive and beneficial era that mankind had ever known.

But what they never identified or challenged was the opposing monetary rule of conduct advocated by their Policy Makers: the government that aims to acquire wealth must confiscate it—or counterfeit its equivalent in paper claims.

Evolution of the Theory

The gold standard limited artificial *monetary* expansion and in doing so, it limited artificial *economic* expansion. The Policy Maker considered this great virtue of the gold standard to be its major vice.

The Policy Maker saw that artificial monetary expansion had led to economic booms. He also saw that at the end of every artificial boom there occurred a financial panic and depression.

The Policy Maker ignored the cause of financial panics, he saw only their effects—bank runs and the demand for gold redemption. He ignored the cause of economic depressions, he saw only that the boom had ended. Reversing cause and effect, the Policy Maker concluded: eliminate gold redemption and the financial panics would stop; eliminate the gold standard and the boom would never end.

The Policy Maker had to make another major move toward institutionalizing government intervention and his theories of artificial monetary expansion into the American way of life: he had to divorce the idea of *national* production from the idea of *individual* productivity.

Ignoring the fact that the individual was the source of production, he convinced men that in the name of "social prosperity," government could and should "stimulate" the economy and "encourage" national production; while at the same time he advocated income taxation to penalize individuals for being productive. Implicit in this doctrine is the idea that production is a gift of the state, the result of government guidance, and that individual productivity is a sin, the result of human greed.

Men were subtly offered a false alternative: the "permission" to produce and be taxed directly through government confiscation; or the "luxury" of an artificial boom, to be taxed indirectly through inflation.

The American people rejected both alternatives (and still do today) yet saw no other acceptable course of action —the intellectual opposition was still too weak to provide them with one. Thus, by default, they accepted both alternatives "to a limited degree." An income tax should be levied "only on those who could afford it," while the government "should steer the economy on a prosperous course."

How was the economy to be "steered?" By supplying unending paper reserves to a regimented banking system and compelling bankers to keep interest rates artificially low. But in 1913 it was too early to sell the public on the "virtues" of the direct confiscation of gold. But the time was "right" for the takeover of the banking system. A monetary revolution was in store for America.

Fractional Reserve Banking

In the name of "economizing" gold (which allegedly was not in sufficient supply to be used as money), Policy Makers advocated a fractional reserve system. A fractional reserve system would *by law* set a ratio at which gold must be held to back legal tender notes. While fractional reserve banking had always been practiced by banks and condoned by governments, the Policy Maker formalized and legitimized it through the Federal Reserve System domestically and the gold exchange standard internationally.

What the Federal Reserve System and the gold exchange standard had in common was a central banking system that used as reserves both gold and money substitutes (such as demand deposits, fractionally backed Federal Reserve notes, commercial paper theoretically convertible into various commodities, and government securities backed by the taxing power of the government). These reserves—gold and the money substitutes—served as a *base* for monetary expansion.

Gold was no longer the sole reserve asset: it was now supplemented by paper reserves. The government exercising a monopoly on the issuance of paper money could designate what should comprise the monetary reserves. Hence, redemption was now not only in gold, but also in money substitutes. In this way a pyramiding of money and credit expansion could take place without the automatic limitations imposed by the gold standard.

By the 1920s the Federal Reserve System had grown and increased its power and controls, which enabled it to increase the money supply and reduce interest rates for longer periods of time. The Federal Reserve Board succeeded in implementing its easy money policies. The problem now was that money and credit became so easy to obtain that it spilled over into the stock market and other investment areas.

The government became alarmed over this wild speculation, raised interest rates sharply, and slammed on the monetary brakes—but it was too late. The day came (that inevitable day) in October 1929 when the Law of Causality presented its bill.

Men found that their profits were merely paper profits, that their prosperity was an illusion. The stock market crashed. Men suddenly realized that on the other side of the coin of credit there existed debt. Industries fought to become "liquid"; everyone tried to get hard cash. But the hard cash—the gold—was insufficient to cover the outstanding claims.

The Great Depression

The Policy Maker succeeded in implementing his theories, yet all of the consequences that his theories were to have eliminated confronted him once again—this time to a far greater degree. This was the *Great* Depression; this was the monetary crisis that not only forced an entire national banking system to close its doors, but was of *international* dimensions. The dollar was in trouble not only at home, but also abroad. What to do?

The Policy Maker had the "answer." He viciously condemned gold and capitalism for causing the crisis and advocated even greater policies of money and credit expansion in order to "stimulate" the economy; more government controls, more government regulations, more and higher taxes were the "answer." Men were asked to give up their gold patriotically in order to save the nation's credit. It was a time of emergency, so Americans complied. They did not know that they would never see their gold again, that taxes would continue to rise higher and higher, and that inflation would become a way of life.

The Policy Maker had to do a lot of talking to convince men of the "evils" of gold and capitalism. He had to do a lot of talking, but when he was finished, men were convinced. They were convinced that nothing less than the direct confiscation of wealth and a vigorous credit expansion could save the nation.

Devaluation in 1934

In 1934, Franklin D. Roosevelt with one stroke of the pen confiscated the entire gold stock of America. When government held the gold and the citizens held only paper, the government reduced the value of the paper by over 40 percent, raising the official dollar "price" of its gold holdings. (The Policy Maker had learned that credit expansion meant debt creation, but showed governments how to default on their debts by devaluing the monetary unit in relation to gold and other currencies.)

The United States was now on a fiat standard domestically, and again in the name of "economizing" gold, the government printed new money against its total stock of newly acquired gold. Deficit spending became a way of life and government borrowing became so insatiable that any mention of paying off the national debt was smeared as unrealistic and regressive in light of the "virtues" of continued monetary expansion. (The Policy

156 / *Paul Stevens*

Maker had learned that borrowing meant debt accumulation, but showed the government how to *"amortize"* its debts by charging its citizens in direct and hidden taxes.)

Domestically the fiat standard has failed miserably. It was designed to "economize" gold and provide a stable dollar. Since 1913, the dollar has lost approximately 75 percent of its purchasing power. The fractional gold cover has been progressively reduced, and transferred to cover obligations abroad. That gold reserve has been reduced from $25 billion to $10 billion through demands for redemption by foreign governments which finally forced the United States to close the doors of its central bank. (The central bank was supposed to be a bank of last resort. The run on the Treasury's gold amounts to the largest and most prolonged bank run in the history of any nation.)

Bretton Woods

Meanwhile, internationally, in 1944 a "new" system was established—the Bretton Woods system. During the Bretton Woods era Policy Makers adopted policies of vigorous credit expansion as a panacea for the world's problems. The instrument of credit used was the dollar. In its role as reserve currency, the dollar was considered "as good as gold" and served as a supplement to world gold reserves. In the name of world liquidity, dollars would be furnished as needed to replenish and build up world reserves. The dollar was envisioned as a stable yet ever-expanding reserve currency.

In this spirit, dollars poured forth on demand via U.S. deficits in the form of foreign aid, loans, and military expenditures. Foreign demand for dollars never ceased, nor did the expansion of money and credit, until the world found itself in the midst of an inflationary spiral which turned to recession and ended in an international monetary crisis: the dollar inconvertible, dropping in value, an undesirable credit instrument and ineffective reserve currency.

The dollar was again devalued, while gold soared in value, reaching new highs. And through all this, Policy Makers have been screaming the same old theories: "Gold is a barbarous relic! It ought to be eliminated completely! What we need is *more* liquidity . . . *more* money and credit!"

What more can the Policy Maker do?

The Theory Projected

There is a causal link between history and future events—the link is theory.

A theory is a policy or set of ideas proposed as the basis for human action. To the extent that a theory furthers man's life it is a practical basis for human action and therefore a good theory. To the extent that a theory destroys man's life it is impractical, self-defeating, and therefore a bad theory.

A sound monetary theory, if employed, will facilitate trade and economic growth, while an unsound monetary theory will lead to monetary crises and economic disruptions.

The Policy Maker has been charged with providing theoretical ammunition to government. To the Policy Maker's great discredit he has learned nothing about monetary theory in the last two centuries, save how to employ more sophisticated techniques of credit expansion. He has rejected the lessons of history through self-induced blindness and has made himself deaf and dumb to rational economic analysis. He sees nothing except his precious theories of artificial monetary expansion.

Today's Policy Maker sees himself as participating in an evolution of the international monetary system comparable in "importance" to the role his intellectual ancestor played in evolving the gold standard into the gold exchange standard. And if by evolution the Policy Maker means a series of changes in a given direction, this is a correct description of his role. But it is the *wrong* direction. And it has been the wrong direction for over a century.

Given the monetary theories held by today's Policy Makers who are concerned with international monetary reform, one can expect a change only in the method and degree of monetary expansion—not a change in direction.

Each time the Policy Maker has seen his monetary theories implemented he has blinded himself to their effects. Each time a monetary or economic crisis has occurred he has refused to identify the cause, blaming it on the so-called "business cycle" which he insists is an inherent weakness within capitalism and which invariably causes depressions. But there is no such thing as a "business cycle" that causes depressions—only a cycle of continuous government intervention into the economy, providing newly printed money that causes inflation, malinvestment, over-consumption, the misallocation of resources—distortions and mistakes that, when liquidated, are called depressions.

There is nothing in the nature of capitalism and the free market to cause such crises. If economic history has tended to repeat itself, it is because the Policy Maker has been guiding human action and government policies along a circular theoretical course that has been tried and has failed—again and again and again.

"If at First You Don't Succeed . . ."

The spectacle of billions of inconvertible dollars frozen in the vaults of central banks has brought on cries of condemnation over the dollar's credibility as a reserve currency.

The Policy Maker's theory of a stable yet artificially ever-expanding reserve currency has failed. Policy Makers are willing to admit this freely. The failure, of course, was not theirs—it was "all gold's fault." The Policy Maker avoids dealing with the problem by insisting that there is too little gold in existence instead of too many claims to gold outstanding.

The "solution" to the problem (if the Policy Maker remains consistent) will be to evolve the international monetary system from a system in which an ever-expanding reserve *currency* provided the world with credit and liquidity, to a system in which an ever-expanding reserve *"asset"* will fill that role. Like the dollar, this reserve "asset" will amount to circulating debt, i.e. something owed rather than something owned. It will be a non-market instrument, deriving its acceptability from government cooperation and decree, "immune from the laws of the free market and outside the reach of greedy speculators."

Where will this "asset" come from? Under the Bretton Woods system, dollar reserves were furnished by the U.S. central bank. Both the bank and the "asset" failed. The next step is to create a *world* bank (a larger bank of last resort) controlled by an international organization (the IMF) with the power to create a new "asset," independent of any single government's monetary policy.

As a supplement to gold and like the dollar before it, this "asset" should be a credit instrument. Unlike the dollar, it would have the backing of an entire world of central banks. The "asset" should be ever-expanding and should provide both liquidity and stability. In short, "as good as gold."

The SDR: "As Good as Gold" Again!

Special Drawing Rights (SDR's), or "paper gold" as it is sometimes referred to by those who can keep a straight face, was introduced to the international monetary system in 1967. It was a time when the dollar was under suspicion and gold was increasingly demanded.

In order to "economize" gold, the IMF issued a new reserve "asset" (SDR's) to supplement gold and take pressure off the dollar. The SDR is a bookkeeping entry, defined in gold yet non-convertible into gold. It serves the same function as gold since it is a reserve, but unlike gold, it can be created by a stroke of the pen.

U.S. Policy Makers have chosen the SDR as the reserve "asset" most likely to succeed in replacing gold. But just as the dollar was supposed to be as good as gold and was not, the SDR, even if made tangible and convertible into gold and/or other currencies, will suffer the same demise.

The Policy Maker has chosen to ignore the fact that there is no fundamental difference between an artificially ever-expanding reserve currency and an artificially ever-expanding reserve "asset"—both are inflationary and therefore self-destructive.

But the real threat is not that the SDR may fail as the dollar did in bringing monetary stability. The threat is in the damage SDR's can do if developed within a formal system. Just as the dollar replaced gold as the primary asset, SDR's have a very real potential for further diminishing the role of gold, and in doing so changing the entire nature and inflationary potential of the IMF.

The most controversial question in monetary reform today centers around the respective roles of gold and SDR's. While the United States has taken an anti-gold position, France has been said to have taken a pro-gold position in opposition to U.S. proposals. But if one checks the theories held by the Policy Makers of the governments involved, the "pro-gold" opposition looks absurdly weak.

The Mythical Pro-gold Governments

The United States wants a lesser role for gold, holding that SDR's can serve as a measurement of currency value, act as a credit instrument, earn interest, and absorb dollars. In effect the U.S. position would eliminate gold's major role without eliminating gold. SDR's would not only become the standard of value for all currencies, they would replace gold as redemption instruments.

The "opposition" (mainly France) wants gold as the major reserve asset in which all currency values are measured. While the United States proposes that excess dollars be "absorbed" by an IMF issuance of SDR's, France proposes instead that the official "price" of gold be raised sufficiently high to convert excess dollars in central banks.

Superficially, it would appear that there are two opposing positions being taken: one anti-gold, one pro-gold. However, both positions are anti-gold standard, hence anti-gold as a reserve asset.

A gold standard requires that governments limit the currencies they print to the supply of gold they possess—and this is considered out of the question by today's government leaders. They insist on the "right" to inflate. "Pro-gold" European governments have, time and time again, inflated their currencies, then devalued. To advocate arbitrarily raising the "price" of gold is as much an attempt to use gold as a fiat reserve asset as is the U.S. position.

While the United States would increase reserves by printing "assets" to cover present and future money and credit needs, France would increase reserves by raising the "price" of gold to cover the artificial money and credit *previously* created. And this is the common denominator that links the two apparently opposing positions: their basic agreement, in principle, that the artificial creation of money and credit is essential to any monetary system. Disagreement only arises over the *method* to be used in dealing with excessive monetary expansion, i.e., *debt*.

There are no pro-gold governments in existence today, only pro-inflation governments. The difference between governments is only in the degree of monetary expansion and the freedom of gold ownership a government permits.

"Amortize" or Default: the False Alternative

So, basically, monetary reform boils down to the following two alternatives: the "pro-gold" countries advocate *defaulting* on foreign debts via devaluation; the "anti-gold" countries advocate *"amortizing"* foreign debts via artificial reserve expansion. (The kind of "amortization" that is consistent with the Policy Makers' theories amounts to a method of constantly refinancing government debt below the market rate of interest. Given the past record of government, the principal may never be repaid in full or in real money terms.)

The third alternative is simply to not *create* debts that governments are unable or unwilling to repay. The third alternative is for governments to stop arbitrarily creating debt instruments such as the dollar in its role as reserve currency, and the SDR. These instruments and the currencies printed against them invariably depreciate and cause monetary crises. The third alternative would mean returning to the gold standard which, in today's "enlightened" era and within our "evolving" economic structure, is considered "passé" and "old-fashioned."

Thus, in the present political context, monetary reform will consist of devaluation (and/or revaluation more recently) and default on debts, or artificial reserve expansion and the "amortization" of debts or, more probably, a combination of both.

What is the difference between default and "amortization?"

Consider the example of a man whose expenditures have for some time been exceeding his income. He has in effect been running a deficit. He finds himself with more short-term claims against him than he has liquid assets. If he refuses to liquidate assets and finds a way to default on his short-term claims, the loss falls directly on his creditors. (When governments default on *their* creditors, they call it devaluation.)

But what if the man refinances his short-term obligations by printing IOU's far in excess of his assets, and offers interest on this new "medium of exchange?" What if this new "medium of exchange" is then used as an "asset" by creditors who, in turn, print IOU's against it and distribute these as direct claims to goods?

Here the loss falls on all those who are in the domain of the counterfeiters, and who must suffer the effects of artificially rising prices. (When the government thus creates fiat money in this way, they call the process "amortization.")

From this example, the following conclusion can be drawn relative to governments: any form of debt default falls squarely on the shoulders of the creditors, i.e., on the citizens of creditor governments. Any form of debt "amortization," however, falls indiscriminately on the shoulders of all those individuals within the monetary sphere of those governments participating in an international monetary system of debt "amortization."

No ring of international counterfeiters has ever been, or could ever be, more of a threat to individuals and their wealth than is the IMF in its move toward international monetary "reform."

The Frightening Prospect of an International Debt

In the past, devaluation and default on excessive debt has been the method most used to eliminate debt. But, given an international system of artificial reserve expansion, the issuance of credit and the "amortization" of debts may be expected to give rise to the specter of an *international debt*.

The possibility of an international debt is not a pleasant one to contemplate. Like a national debt that continues to grow without restraint through continuous refinancing, an international debt would soon become uncontrollable and self-perpetuating.

The victims of such debt "amortization" must ultimately be individuals: taxpayers to the degree that the debt is financed directly or repaid; consumers to the degree that the debt is refinanced indirectly through the inflationary method of money creation; or creditors if and when (or to the degree that) the debt is ultimately repudiated.

Given the choice between "amortization" and default as methods of dealing with the problem of debt, and given the inflationary policies that governments are determined to follow, it makes little difference what kind of monetary "reform" is implemented. Our monetary authorities are only haggling over who should be the victims of their debt creation—foreigners or nationals.

Rational and morally concerned individuals will not cheer their government for shifting the burden of their debt onto foreign citizens through the process of debt default and devaluation. On the other hand, given debt "amortization," the citizens of all countries will suffer the inevitable result of more taxation and more inflation.

Thus an individual will pay taxes, and on top of that the hidden tax of inflation for *domestic programs,* and on top of that an inflationary tax for *world expenditures,* and on top of that the inflationary tax for *interest* on all inflationary debts both domestic and international.

Toward an International Fiat Reserve System

It is not an easy thing to eliminate gold from a monetary system and replace it with the continuously depreciating promises of paper money and paper "assets." All such money substitutes at one time derived their value from and were dependent on the market or exchange value of commodities.

It takes a lot of time and a lot of talking to convince men to accept artificial values as distinguished from the market-determined values in exchange. In America, Policy Makers have had nearly two centuries in which to propagate their monetary theories and institutionalize them within the policies of state. The result has been a slow erosion and obscuring of gold's role in the monetary systems of man.

The monetary system that lies at the end of the Policy Maker's theories is an international fiat reserve system. The foot in the door that opens the way to this system is the SDR.

The U.S. proposal to replace gold with the SDR amounts to just such a proposal. (Whether or not "SDR" is the final name given to a fiat reserve asset is unimportant. What is important is simply whether that asset derives its value realistically or arbitrarily.) But the United States knows that governments will not simply give up their gold overnight. And while it is true the so-called "pro-gold" countries have no intention of giving up their gold, the role of gold can be so diminished within the future monetary system that it will no longer serve as a protection against artificial monetary expansion, even to the limited degree that it has in recent years. An "opposition" that is in basic agreement with U.S. theories of artificial credit expansion cannot be expected to properly defend gold's role in any future international monetary system.

If there is to be a "meeting of the minds" on international monetary reform, it will come through compromise—and that compromise must lessen gold's role in the future. Worse, if this compromise is achieved, it will establish an unprecedented potential for world inflation.

International Demonetization

What will be the nature of this compromise? Given the theories of world Policy Makers, the most probable compromise would be to issue, as "legal tender" notes, SDR's backed by a *fractional* amount of gold.

The effect of such an agreement will concede to the IMF the power to create reserves and set in motion the unrestricted workings of an *international* fractional reserve system.

Just as gold was demonetized in the United States through the method of fractional reserve banking, the Policy Makers will attempt to demonetize gold internationally.

A sequence of events typical of what one might expect from Policy Makers would be for them to advocate the establishment of a central bank (the IMF) that has the power to create reserve assets, define the asset in gold to give it credibility (fractionally backing the asset with a percentage of gold) and, in the name of "economizing" gold, increase SDR allotments, thereby reducing and eventually eliminating the gold backing, thus facilitating the constant increase in fiat reserves.

Ultimately this system would eliminate any objective limitations on monetary expansion, thereby surrendering monetary policy into the collective hands of a world body the monetary heads of which would subjectively decide which nations will be given the "special right" to consume goods and at whose expense.

Simply Repetitious

This is not a prediction of coming events. It is simply an example of the methods Policy Makers would most likely advocate in order to achieve their goal. Notice that there is nothing innovative about the method of creating a fiat instrument, arbitrarily decreeing its value by force, then proceeding through fractional reserve banking and monetary expansion to systematically undermine the acceptability it had enjoyed by reason of its gold backing. It has all been done before.

These men are not innovators. They are simply repetitious! They would be laughable if they weren't so dangerous. But today's Policy Makers are dangerous. They have the power of government force behind all the theories they propagate. And at the end of their theories awaits chaos.

Given today's political context, an international fiat reserve system must ultimately add to massive world inflation as governments are inclined to spend more and more. This must lead to the eventual collapse of the international monetary system and with it the economies of the world.

The Real Meaning of Monetary Reform

Monetary crises are not born from nature, they are made—man-made.

As long as governments continue to adopt policies of inflationary finance, the monetary systems of the world will be in perpetual disintegration. This disintegration will lead to crises of greater scope and intensity, recurring at shorter intervals, while the meetings on monetary reform become a way of life as Policy Makers offer only variations of their destructive and futile theories.

As long as governments continue their policies of artificial monetary expansion there can be no such thing as monetary reform. To reform means to abandon those policies which have proven to be unjust and incorrect. *Fundamental* monetary reform means that governments would have to abandon their policies of inflationary finance.

The *essence* of contemporary monetary policy is the employment of inflationary finance, which means injustice to individuals who must bear the brunt of the default and "amortization" of government debt, and the continuous depreciation in the value of their currencies. Further, it means that individuals will be forced to suffer the unnecessary and harmful effects of continuous recessions and depressions.

Until fundamental reform is achieved, the individual will remain the source of government financing. One can easily see that the source is being more and more exploited as governments resort to greater and more extensive policies of artificial monetary expansion.

If fundamental reform does not occur, it is only a matter of time until individuals and private property are squandered in an inflationary system of waste.

In the last analysis, real monetary reform must consist of returning to a gold standard. But there are preconditions to be met before a gold standard can be established as a lasting monetary system.

Men must understand what money is. They must rediscover why gold is the most effective medium of exchange and means of saving. And men must discover what money is not. They must understand that by accepting a monetary unit of value by decree, they are not only condoning theft, but are sanctioning the instrument of their own monetary and economic destruction.

When men have understood this, they will want to return to the gold standard.

But the gold standard cannot survive in an economy mixed with socialist controls and vaguely defined individual freedoms. Men must rediscover the virtues of the gold standard; and men will not rediscover the virtues of the gold standard until they rediscover the virtues of capitalism. Men will not rediscover the virtues of capitalism until they identify the nature of man's rights and the injustices of government-initiated force and coercion.

If the gold standard is to return to this country, it will return on the wings of capitalism and not before.

If one wishes to fight for economic and monetary stability, one must also fight for capitalism. If one wishes to fight for capitalism, one must fight for man's rights. If one wishes to engage in this fight, the battle lines are clear: one must engage in an *intellectual* battle to displace the theories held by his intellectual adversaries—the advocates of policies based on coercion.

III. THE WISDOM OF THE
FOUNDING FATHERS

Fiat and the Founding Fathers

by Elgin Groseclose

In this bicentennial year, it is paradoxical that with all the reverence being addressed to the Constitution by the courts, Congress, and presidential aspirants, no one has come forward to challenge the Constitutionality of our money system.

The importance of such a re-examination is emphasized by a recent Yankelovich survey reporting that the issue of greatest concern among voters was inflation (53 percent). Inflation is obviously a problem which has eluded the skill of our money managers, working under prevailing monetary theory, and has defied the edicts of Congress to resolve.

On August 17, 1787, the Constitutional Convention, sitting as a Committee of the Whole, discussed a draft article defining the powers of Congress under the projected new Constitution. A portion of the draft read, "Congress shall have power . . . to coin money, emit bills of credit, regulate the value thereof . . . ."

Gouverneur Morris, delegate from Pennsylvania, highly regarded as a financier, an associate of Robert Morris, who had been largely responsible for the successful financing of the Revolution, rose to propose an amendment. The amendment, as James Madison recorded in his *Notes on the Constitutional Convention,* the principal record of the proceedings, was to strike the words "emit bills of credit." In 1787 language, bills of credit were synonymous with paper money.

"In no country of Europe" a delegate noted, "is paper money legal tender but only gold and silver coin." He had no need to recall the flagrant paper money emissions of the first Continental Congress, which by 1781 had totaled an estimated $200 million, an enormous sum for the times, and which had fallen to a discount of 99 percent before Robert Morris stopped their emission.

The late Dr. Groseclose was head of Groseclose, Williams & Associates, financial and investment consultants of Washington, D.C., and executive director of the Institute for Monetary Research, Inc. This article appeared in the October 1976 issue of *The Freeman.*

There was little debate. The offending language was removed by almost unanimous vote. It was clearly the intention of the framers of the Constitution that paper should not be allowed as legal tender in the new Union. To reinforce this conviction, the Convention enacted a provision forbidding the member states of the Union to emit paper money (bills of credit) or to declare as legal tender anything but gold and silver coin.

In 1831, Albert Gallatin, who had served Jefferson and Madison as Secretary of the Treasury (1801-1814) declared that "it necessarily follows that nothing but gold and silver coin can be made legal tender," and Daniel Webster in a speech in the Senate, in 1836, proclaimed, "Most unquestionably there is no legal tender, and there can be no legal tender in this country but gold and silver. . . ."

While the idea was already being debated that the supply of money should correspond to the needs of trade and some political economists argued that sovereign states could declare their paper money legal tender, the framers of the Constitution held to the view that money should consist of something substantial, and that if paper were issued as an expedient it should always be representative of, and redeemable in, coin.

From this accepted principle, built into the foundation of the American political system, modern practice has so far diverged that money today consists of neither gold nor silver coin, but only a degraded alloy together with a vast amount of paper money irredeemable in any metal. John Law, the Scottish financier who became Comptroller General of France, in a disastrous experiment tried to make paper money representative of the wealth of France. What circulates today as money is not evidence of wealth but paradoxically the very opposite, the absence of wealth, that is to say, debt, which is no more than a pious hope for later possession of wealth.

"Freeing up the Money Supply"

How did this revolution occur? During the Civil War Congress, as a war measure, authorized the issuance of circulating notes declared to be legal tender. The action was stoutly debated and, while it was eventually approved by the Supreme Court, the principle continued to govern that paper money, unless fully redeemable in lawful money, that is gold or silver coin, was allowable only as a recourse of national emergency. It was not until the Federal Reserve Act in 1913 that the view became authoritative that circulating notes could be issued against evidences of debt. Until 1934 such notes could be regarded, in a sense, as representative of metal, since they were redeemable in gold, but thereafter irredeemable by U.S. citizens, and they were never full legal tender until 1965. After 1971, they became completely inconvertible in metal. At present the circulating media of this country consist of some $9 billion in degraded coin and $77 billion of Federal Reserve notes, plus a small amount of other notes.

Source of Inflation

The consequences of this revolution will be discussed later. For a moment let us look at the intellectual atmosphere in which it was nurtured. As a consequence of a sudden collapse of credit in 1907, leading to what has been called a money panic, the Federal Reserve System came into being with the object of adjusting the supply of money to finance the seasonal trade of a then mainly agricultural economy. This limited concept of "flexible currency" was soon expanded under the necessities of World War I when the Federal Reserve notes and credit were used to finance the government.

In 1923, the Federal Reserve managers concluded that the System's power should be used in the interest of a stable price level, under the theory that as the production of goods rises the money supply must also rise at comparable rate to provide business with the means of payment. The theory flew in the face of the fact that a prime purpose of technology is to make goods more abundant, and presumably cheaper in order to be more widely distributed. It also overlooked the fact that the technology of money was being improved, through banking and credit procedures, so that a given supply of money could serve a greater volume of transactions.

Nevertheless, the theory became a justification for a steady expansion of the money supply, some economists advocating a regular, mathematical rise in the money supply regardless of the rate of physical growth. So embedded, in fact, has the idea become that both the Democratic presidential candidate, Governor Carter, and such a conservative Republican as Secretary of the Treasury William Simon, have indicated that they regard a monetary inflation of three percent annually as normal.

The use of debt money created by the Federal Reserve was further expanded by the Employment Act of 1946, by which the federal government assumed responsibility for providing employment opportunities for all.

Purchasing Power Theory of Money

In discharging its responsibilities under the Employment Act of 1946, the managers of the System undertook a still deeper intrusion of federal authority into management of the economy. Heretofore money had been considered to consist only of the official circulating media. The System now undertook to redefine money not in terms of its substance but of its attributes. Money was purchasing power, and since bank deposits were a form of purchasing power, the System now began to treat money as the sum of the circulation plus demand deposits. This purchasing power was called M1 to distinguish it from the official circulation, known as M. The Federal Reserve is able to influence the amount of such purchasing power by its authority over the reserves which member banks of the System must carry.

It now became apparent that there were other forms of purchasing power besides that represented by circulating notes and coin and demand deposits, and to extend its authority over the economy the System developed the concept of M2 consisting of circulating media and demand deposits (M1) plus savings bank deposits, since a savings bank deposit can obviously be converted on notice to purchasing power by means of a withdrawal or transfer to a checking account.

The Insubstantiality of Money

What is universal about all these forms of money—M, M1 , M2—is that they are forms of debt rather than substance. Bank deposits represent the bank's liabilities to depositors, secured in turn by various liabilities of others to the banks, plus a minute amount of physical assets. The liabilities consist of loan obligations of bank customers and investments, which in turn consist principally of debt instruments, that is, corporate bonds and U.S. Treasury obligations, and deposits at the Federal Reserve Bank, which in turn are obligations of that institution. The bank may also hold a small amount of physical assets, consisting of bank premises and furnishings, and real estate acquired in liquidation of foreclosed loans, and in course of sale. The bank may also hold a small amount of cash, but this cash, consisting of Federal Reserve notes and coin is again in form of obligation, unless coin is considered a physical asset to the extent of the market value of the metal contained.

The consequences of this transferring the concept of money from substance to purchasing power is to enter an uncharted realm of theory, in which the power of government to intervene in individual affairs is open to unlimited expansion. The idea of a government of limited or delegated powers disappears. Thus, the question of the extent to which credit cards are a form of money now engages the attention of the System managers, since credit cards are a form of purchasing power.

But there are other forms more elusive. Thus, if A, a grocer gives his doctor a note of hand for services rendered, the note represents purchasing power in that A thereby acquired services without equivalent goods or services in payment. If the doctor in turn returns the note to A in payment of merchandise, he has used purchasing power that has escaped the statistics of the Federal Reserve. In short, any good or service that has exchange value is a form of purchasing power, and to put all this purchasing power under the control of the Federal Reserve is to give that agency a control or influence over the livelihood activities of the country, the extent of which is yet to be tested.

The Consequences of the New Money

We may now examine briefly the consequences of this departure from the monetary views of the Founding Fathers. In only 15 years, 1960-1975, the Federal Reserve notes in circulation more than doubled, from $27¼ billion to $77 billion, and coin in circulation from $2½ billion to $9 billion. In the same interval the purchasing power fostered by the System in the form of demand deposits, so-called M1, increased from $141 billion to $295 billion.

The flooding of the country with such an immense amount of new purchasing power had its inevitable effect on prices, with the index for consumer commodities doubling from 88 to 167.

The virus of inflation, feeding on the lush growth of paper money, was not limited to this country, but has become a worldwide plague, a disease carried by the U.S. dollar and the American doctrine of central banking into every corner of the planet. Utilizing a device first developed and approved by the Genoa Conference of 1922, that the debts of a rich country could be counted as the assets of a poor, impecunious governments set up central banks with power to issue notes against U.S. Treasury obligations. Since the Federal Reserve notes and deposits were until 1971 redeemable in gold, such obligations were treated as the equivalent of gold.

Regrettably, the practice proved its own undoing. At the end of World War II the U.S. Treasury held about $25 billion in gold (at $35 an ounce), but U.S. fiscal recklessness, inordinate foreign aid expenditures, and excessive credit issues domestically, led the shrewder foreign governments to convert some of their U.S. Treasury debt into gold, until by 1968 the U.S. stock had diminished to less than $11 billion (at $35 an ounce). The accelerating weakness of the dollar in the succeeding years required the Treasury to put restraints on the outflow, and in 1971 redemption ceased altogether. The consequence has been a worldwide currency debacle with exchanges unstable and great banks in bankruptcy from foreign exchange losses.

Consequences—Mathematical and Moral

Space does not permit an examination of the economic and social consequences of continued inflation of prices from the issue of fiat purchasing power and they are too evident in the mounting unrest and dissatisfaction with the political system to require description. It is necessary only to add that the unwillingness of governments to deal decisively with inflation is a leading cause of the disintegration of U.S.-European political influence in world affairs.

The reason for this political impotence lies at a deeper level than the economy. It goes profoundly to the realm of morals. Money is rightly called the lifeblood of commerce. When the blood is corrupt the whole body is diseased. There is an essential corruption and moral debility in a monetary system that permits a government to spend and distribute largess obtained without taxation, by a process so simple as a bookkeeping entry or the operation of a printing press, thereby to create purchasing power that enters the market in competition with purchasing power gained through the efforts of human labor and ingenuity.

Alexander del Mar quotes Antoninus Augustus: "Money had more to do with the distemper of the Roman empire than the Huns or the Vandals," and the system of fiat money into which this country has fallen, in violation of the Constitution, may be the distemper to which this country may soon succumb.

John Witherspoon: Disciple of Freedom

by Robert G. Bearce

"There is not a single instance in history," declared Reverend John Witherspoon in 1776, "in which civil liberty was lost, and religious liberty preserved entire. If therefore we yield up our temporal property, we at the same time deliver the conscience into bondage. "[1] Speaking as a minister, Reverend Witherspoon understood the inseparable tie between political freedom and spiritual freedom. Like John Adams and Patrick Henry, he was an outspoken Patriot, advocating independence from Great Britain.

Dr. Witherspoon is remembered mainly for his tenure as President of the College of New Jersey (Princeton University) and for having been the only clergyman to sign the *Declaration of Independence*. His truly important contribution to American liberty and independence, though, was revealed by his stalwart labors as a member of the Continental Congress. Elected in 1776, he served his last term in 1782. During this period, he attempted to bring sound economic wisdom to Congressional deliberations. Unfortunately for the struggling Thirteen States, his astute views and timely admonitions were often rejected. Consequently, America had to fight both the British Army and the evils of inflation and price-fixing.

Eighteen years after the War for Independence was finally won, Witherspoon published his *Essay on Money,* "As a medium of commerce; with remarks on the advantages and disadvantages of paper admitted into general circulation. "[2] This excellent work gives hindsight, insight, and foresight into economic problems—the same problems faced by the United States in the 20th century. Writing about the general topic of money, Witherspoon also gives us a clear understanding of "commerce"—free exchange and free enterprise.

"Let us then begin," he says, "by considering what gave rise to money, and what is its nature and use? If there were but one man upon the earth, he would be obliged to prepare a hut for his habitation, to dig roots for his

Mr. Bearce is a free-lance writer in Houston, Texas. This article first appeared in the May 1977 issue of *The Freeman*.

sustenance, to provide skins or fig leaves for his covering, &c. in short, to do every thing for himself. If but one or two more were joined with him, it would soon be found that one of them would be more skillful in one sort of work, and another in a different; so that common interest would direct them, each to apply his industry to what he could do best and soonest; to communicate the surplus of what he needed himself to that sort of work to the others, and receive of their surplus in return.

"This directly points out to us, that a barter of commodities, or communication of the fruits of industry, is the first principle or rather indeed constitutes the essence of commerce. As society increases, the partition of employments is greatly diversified; but still the fruits of well directed industry, or the things necessary and useful in life are what only can be called wealth."[3]

A Preference for Gold

As a rugged Scotsman by birth, Reverend Witherspoon had an appreciation for gold. His distaste for printed bills was founded upon firm economic judgment, and he was ready to defend precious metals.

"It is likely some will say, What is the intrinsic value of gold and silver? They are not wealth; they are but the sign or representative of commodities. Superficial philosophers, and even some men of good understanding not attending to the nature of currency, have really said so. What is gold, say some, the value is all in the fancy; you can neither eat nor wear it; it will neither feed, clothe nor warm you. Gold, say others, as to intrinsic value, is not so good as iron which can be applied to many more useful purposes.

"These persons have not attended to the nature of commercial value, which is a compound ratio of its use and scarceness. If iron were as rare as gold, it would probably be as valuable, perhaps more so. How many instances are there of things, which, though a certain proportion of them is not only valuable, but indispensably necessary to life itself, yet which from their abundance have no commercial value at all.

"Take for examples air and water. People do not bring these to market, because they are in superabundant plenty. But let any circumstances take place that render them rare, and difficult to be obtained, and their value immediately rises above all computation. What would one of those who were stifled in the black hole at Calcutta, have given to get but near a window for a little air? And what will the crew of a ship at sea, whose water is nearly expended, give for a fresh supply?"[4]

The Weakness of Paper

Witherspoon understood the stability of gold just as he saw the weakness of paper. Why should nations fear printed bills as legal tender?

"The evil is this: All paper introduced into circulation, and obtaining credit as gold and silver, adds to the quantity of the medium, and thereby . . . increases the price of industry and its fruits."[5]

Today we call it inflation. By "the price of industry and its fruits," Witherspoon meant the higher costs for employment, land, tools, and business expansion. Expenses and prices go up. True profits and income go down. The individual's industry—his daily labor or his business—might bring in more greenbacks, but their value will be shrinking.

"Experience," he warns, "has every where justified the remark, that wherever paper is introduced in large quantities, the gold and silver vanishes universally. The joint sum of gold, silver, and paper current, will exactly represent your whole commodities, and the prices will be accordingly. It is therefore as if you were to fill a vessel brim full, making half the quantity water and the other oil, the last being specifically lightest, will be at the top, and if you add more water, the oil only will run over, and continue running till there is none left.

"How absurd and contemptible then is the reasoning which we of late have seen frequently in print, viz. the gold and silver is going away from us, therefore we must have paper to supply its place. If the gold and silver is indeed going away from us, that is to say, if the balance of trade is much against us, the paper medium has a direct tendency to increase the evil, and send it away by a quicker pace."[6]

"Hence it may be seen, that the resolution of the question, whether it is proper to have paper money at all or not, depends entirely upon another, viz. whether the evil that is done by augmenting the circulating medium, is or is not over-balanced by the facility given to commerce, and the credit given to particular persons, by which their industry and exertions are added to the common stock."[7]

Belief in Freedom Under God

When Reverend Witherspoon came to the Colonies in 1768 to assume the presidency of the College of New Jersey, he brought with him his evangelical Christian faith and a profound intellect. Sharp-minded but humble, he had the gift of aggressive, orderly thought. As a student of the Scriptures, he recognized that God did not compel men to accept Him. Individuals were free to choose or reject obedience to their Creator.

Likewise, he saw that God meant for individuals to have political and economic freedom in the earthly life. Man's temporal rights—"life, liberty, and the pursuit of happiness"—were God-given. Freedom was a matter for one's soul as well as his daily bread. Thus, the Princeton preacher applies the principle of voluntary action and personal choice to commercial enterprises:

"Well! is it agreed that all commerce is founded on a complete contract? . . . One of the essential conditions of a lawful contract, and indeed the first of them, is, that it be *free* and *mutual.* Without this it may be something else, and have some other binding force, but it is not a contract. To make laws therefore, regulating the prices of commodities, or giving nominal value to that which had no value before the law was made, is altering the nature of the transaction altogether.[8]

"Thus we know, that in cities, in case of a fire, sometimes a house, without the consent of its owner, will be destroyed to prevent the whole from being consumed. But if you make a law that I shall be obliged to *sell* my grain, my cattle, or any commodity, at a certain price, you not only do what is unjust and impolitic, but with all respect be it said, you speak nonsense; for I do not *sell* them at all: you take them from me. You are both buyer and seller, and I am the sufferer only.[9]

"I cannot help observing that laws of this kind have an inherent weakness in them: they are not only unjust and unwise, but for the most part impracticable. They are an attempt to apply authority to that which is not its proper object, and to extend it beyond its natural bounds; in both which we shall be sure to fail. The production of commodities must be the effect of industry, inclination, hope, and interest. The first of these is very imperfectly reached by authority, and the other three cannot be reached by it at all.

"Perhaps I ought rather to have said that they cannot be directed by it, but they may be greatly counteracted; as people have naturally a strong disposition to resist force, and to escape from constraint. Accordingly we found in this country, and every other society who ever tried such measures found, that they produced an effect directly contrary to what was expected from them. Instead of producing moderation and plenty, they uniformly produced dearness and scarcity."[10]

With Good Intention

Witherspoon insisted that "tender laws, arming paper, or any thing not valuable in itself with authority are directly contrary to the very first principles of commerce." Regrettably, "many of the advocates for such laws, and many of those who are instrumental in enacting them, do it from pure ignorance, without any bad intention."[11]

Monetary considerations aside, Dr. Witherspoon's observation points to one of the problems still facing the American economy. We have our own government officials, educators, and socio-political writers who in "ignorance, without any bad intention," propose coercive measures in economic matters. They are guided by a humanitarian spirit, but it is an idealism that ignores personal freedom and individual responsibility. Their "ignorance" fosters both economic stagnation and political regimentation.

With regard to attempts at corrupting a nation's currency, Witherspoon observed that "the only thing resembling it in the English history is, James the second coining base metal, and affixing a price to it by proclamation; a project contemptible in the contrivance, and abortive in the execution."[12]

"It seems to me, that those who cry out for emitting paper money by the legislatures, should take some pains to state clearly the difference between this and the European countries, and point out the reasons why it would be serviceable here, and hurtful there."[13] Again, laying aside the specific topic of paper currency, we have a general admonition that should be heeded. Statist-minded politicians and economists in the United States should explain why their own blueprints for a planned economy in America will work any better here than do their socialistic counterparts in Africa, Europe, Asia, or South America.

An Incisive Approach

Although Reverend Witherspoon was not an eloquent speaker, he knew how to present basic truths clearly and forcefully. Serving as a member of Congress during the war, he spent fewer hours preaching from the pulpit. Work in Congress, though, enabled him to demonstrate his clarity of thought and his ability to get to the heart of a problem.

When proposals for price-fixing came up, he protested vigorously—both in speech and print. In 1777 Congress was considering whether or not it should recommend to all the States the "Connecticut Act for Regulating Prices"—a plan already adopted by a convention of four New England States. It would have regulated prices of labor, manufactures, imports and provisions.

Witherspoon voted an emphatic "Nay!" to the "Connecticut Act": "Sir, it is a wise maxim to avoid those things which our enemies wish us to practice ... Remember, laws are not almighty . ... It is beyond the power of despotic princes to regulate the prices of goods ... If we limit *one* article, we must limit everything, and this is impossible."[14]

General Washington also heard from the New Jersey sage on the evils of price-fixing. Describing himself as a "Jersey Farmer," Dr. Witherspoon advised the Commander-in-Chief that several states had already tried to set prices by law. The measures had only made food and supplies even more scarce. "To fix the prices of goods, especially provisions in a market," he wrote, "is as impracticable as it is unreasonable."

Freedom of Exchange

Who, then, should regulate prices? The buyer and seller themselves, without interference from politicians! Freedom of exchange! Freedom for both the consumer and the businessman!

Behind the different attempts at controlling prices was the staggering inflation. An estimated $200 million of paper money had been issued by 1781. State and Continental currency was almost worthless. Paper money was always Witherspoon's thorn in the side. Looking back upon the inflation of the war, he wrote in *Essay on Money:*

"I observe, that to arm such bills with the authority of the state, and make them a legal tender in all payments, is an absurdity so great, that [it] is not easy to speak with propriety upon it. Perhaps it would give offense if I should say, it is an absurdity reserved for American legislatures; no such thing having ever been attempted in the old countries. It has been found, by the experience of ages, that money must have a standard of value, and if any prince or state debase the metal below the standard, it is utterly impossible to make it succeed.[15]

"Why will you make a law to oblige men to take money when it is offered them? Are there any who refuse it when it is good? If it is necessary to force them, does not this system produce a most ludicrous inversion of the nature of things. For two or three years we constantly saw and were informed of creditors running away from their debtors, and the debtors pursuing them in triumph, and paying them without mercy.

"Let us examine this matter a little more fully. Money is the medium of commercial transactions. Money is itself a commodity. Therefore every transaction in which money is concerned, by being given or promised, is strictly and properly speaking, a bargain, or as it is well called in common language, an agreement. To give, therefore, authority or nominal value by law to any money, is interposing by law, in commerce, and is precisely the same thing with laws regulating the prices of commodities, of which, in their full extent, we had sufficient experience during the war. Now nothing can be more radically unjust, or more eminently absurd, than laws of that nature."[16]

A Contractual Arrangement

What is the basis for a productive, creative society? How does free enterprise operate? The ingredients are goods and services, money, freedom, and the willingness of the individual to cooperate voluntarily with his fellow man. Witherspoon does not speak of a need for government compulsion in commerce:

"Among all civilians, the transactions of commerce are ranged under the head of contracts. Without entering into the nicer distinctions of writers upon this subject, it is sufficient for me to say, that commerce, or buying and selling, is found upon that species of contracts that is most formal and complete. They are called in the technical language, *Onerous contracts*, where the proper and just value is supposed to be given or promised, on both sides. That is to say, the person who offers any thing to sale, does it because he has it to spare, and he thinks it would be better for him to have the money, or some other commodity, than what he parts with; and he who buys, in like manner, thinks it would be better for him to receive the commodity, than to retain the money."[17]

Freedom guided Witherspoon's economic beliefs. He traced most economic difficulties to the conflict between freedom and coercion. Times have changed since the publication of the *Essay on Money,* but his wisdom goes beyond the subject of the American monetary system in 1786.

"I must here take the occasion and the liberty of saying, that it were greatly to be wished that those who have in their hands the administration of affairs in the several states of America, would take no measures, either on this, or any other subject, but what are founded upon justice, supported by reason, and warranted to be safe by the experience of former ages, and of other countries. The operation of political causes is as uniform and certain as that of natural causes. And any measure which in itself has a bad tendency, though its effects may not be instantly discernible, and their progress may be but slow, yet it will be infallible; and perhaps the danger will then only appear when a remedy is impossible.

"This is the case, in some degree, with all political measures, without exception, yet I am mistaken if it is not eminently so with respect to commercial dealings. Commerce is excited, directed, and carried on by interest. But do not mistake this, it is not carried on by general universal interest, nor even by well informed national interest, but by immediate, apparent, and sensible personal interest. I must also observe, that there is in mankind a sharpsightedness upon this subject that is quite astonishing.

"All men are not philosophers, but they are generally good judges of their own profit in what is immediately before them, and will uniformly adhere to it. It is not uncommon to see a man who appears to be almost as stupid as a stone, and yet he shall be as adroit and dexterous in making a bargain, or even more so, than a man of the first rate understanding, who probably, for that very reason, is less attentive to trifling circumstances, and less under the government of mean and selfish views."[18]

Today, there is still a "sharp-sightedness" on the part of individuals who are left free to manage their own interests. Our problem lies in the fact that too many politicians believe themselves to be the only possessors of "sharp-sightedness." They reject Witherspoon's faith that men are "good judges of their own profit." They show contempt for the average citizen— his sense of personal accountability, his intelligence, his self-reliance and discipline.

Individual Responsibility

In May 1776, Reverend Witherspoon spoke to the average American on the occasion of the General Fast, a day of fasting and prayer. His sermon, "The Dominion of Providence over the Passions of Men," touched upon both man's spiritual and earthly needs. Besides urging individuals to seek their eternal welfare, he emphasized individual responsibility in the present, temporal life:

"I exhort all who are not called to go into the field to apply themselves with the utmost diligence to works of industry. It is in your power by this means not only to supply the necessities, but to add to the strength of your country. Habits of industry prevailing in a society not only increase its wealth, as their immediate effect, but they prevent the introduction of many vices, and are intimately connected with sobriety and good morals. Idleness is the mother or nurse of almost every vice; and want, which is its inseparable companion, urges men on to the most abandoned and destructive courses. Industry, therefore is a moral duty of the greatest moment, absolutely necessary to national prosperity, and the sure way of obtaining the blessing of God.[19]

"This certainly implies not only abstaining from acts of gross intemperance and excess, but a humility of carriage, a restraint and moderation in all your desires . . . . The riotous and wasteful liver, whose craving appetites make him constantly needy, is and must be subject to many masters, according to the saying of Solomon, 'The borrower is servant to the lender.' But the frugal and moderate person, who guides his affairs with discretion, is able to assist in public counsels by a free and unbiased judgment, to supply the wants of his poor brethren, and sometimes, by his estate, and substance to give important aid to a sinking country."[20]

Reverend Witherspoon preached his sermon during the critical period of our War for Independence. Liberty was in the balance—would Americans be ruled by oppressive government authority or would they be free to accept their just right to "life, liberty, and the pursuit of happiness"?

We are faced with the same question. The true patriot today is one "who guides his affairs with discretion." Not governmental social planning, but *personal responsibility!* The true patriot is the citizen who acts according to his own "free and unbiased judgment." Not the dictates of government, but *individual initiative!*

1. *The Works of the Reverend John Witherspoon* (Philadelphia: W. W. Woodward, 1800), Vol. 11, p. 427, "The Dominion of Providence over the Passions of Men."

2. *The Works of the Reverend John Witherspoon* (second edition: Philadelphia: W.W. Woodward, 1802), Vol. IV, p. 203.

3. *Ibid.,* p. 204.

4. *Ibid.,* p. 210.

5. *Ibid.,* p. 232.

6. *Ibid.,* p. 233.

7. *Ibid.,* p. 234.

8. *Ibid.,* p. 224.

9. *Ibid.,* pp. 244, 245.

10. *Ibid.,* p. 225.

11. *Ibid.,* p. 226.

12. *Ibid.,* p. 235.

13. *Ibid.,* pp. 235, 236.

14. Henry Steele Commager and Richard B. Morris (eds.), *The Spirit of Seventy-Six* (New York: Harper and Row Publishers, 1967), pp. 783-784.

15. *Works* (2nd edition: 1802), *op. cit.,* pp. 222-223.

16. *Ibid.,* p. 223.

17. *Ibid.,* pp. 223-224.

18. *Ibid.,* pp. 241-242.

19. *Works* (1800), *op cit.,* p. 434.

20. *Ibid.,* pp. 435-436.

OTHER REFERENCES:

Varnum Lansing Collins, *President Witherspoon,* 2 vols. (New York: Arno Press and the New York Times, 1969).

Russell T. Hitt (ed.) *Heroic Colonial Christians* (Philadelphia: J.B. Lippincott Company, 1966).

Martha Lou Stohlman, *John Witherspoon—Parson, Politician, Patriot* (Philadelphia: The Westminster Press, 1976).

The Constitution and Paper Money

by Clarence B. Carson

The United States Constitution does not mention paper money by that name. Nor does it refer to paper currency or fiat money in those words.[1] There is only one direct reference to the origins of what we, and they, usually call paper money. It is in the limitations on the power of the states in Article I, Section 10. It reads, "No State shall... emit Bills of Credit...." Paper that was intended to circulate as money but was not redeemable in gold and silver was technically described as bills of credit at that time. The description was (and is) apt. Such paper is a device for expanding the credit of the issuer. There is also an indirect reference to the practice in the same section of the Constitution. It reads, "No State shall...make any Thing but gold and silver Coin a Tender in Payment of Debts...." Legal tender laws, in practice, are an essential expedient for making unredeemable paper circulate as money. Except for the one direct and one indirect reference to the origin and means for circulating paper money, the Constitution is silent on the question.

With such scant references, then, it might be supposed that the makers of the Constitution were only incidentally concerned with the dangers of paper money. That was hardly the case. It loomed large in the thinking of at least some of the men who were gathered at Philadelphia in 1787 at the Constitutional Convention. There were two great objects in the making of a new constitution: one was to provide for a more energetic general government; the other was to restrain the state governments. Moreover, the two objects had a common motive at many points, i.e., to provide a stronger general government which could restrain the states.

Measures to Prevent a Flood of Unbacked Paper Money

One of the prime reasons for restraining the state governments was to prevent their flooding the country with unbacked paper money. James

---

Dr. Carson has written and taught extensively, specializing in American intellectual history. This article appeared in the July 1983 issue of *The Freeman*.

186

Madison, one of the leaders at the convention, declared, in an introduction to his notes on the deliberations there, that one of the defects they were assembled to remedy was that "In the internal administration of the States, a violation of contracts had become familiar, in the form of depreciated paper made a legal tender . . . ."[2] Edmund Randolph, in the introductory remarks preceding the presentation of the Virginia Plan to the convention, declared that when the Articles of Confederation had been drawn "the havoc of paper-money had not been foreseen."[3]

Indeed, as the convention held its sessions, or in the months preceding it, state legislatures were under pressure to issue paper money. Several had already yielded, or taken the initiative, in issuing the unbacked paper. The situation was out of control in Rhode Island, and had been for some time. Rhode Island refused to send delegates to the convention, and the state's reputation was so bad that the delegates there were apparently satisfied to be spared the counsels of her citizens. Well after the convention had got underway, a motion was made to send a letter to New Hampshire, whose delegates were late, urging their attendance. John Rutledge of South Carolina rose to oppose the motion, arguing that he "could see neither the necessity nor propriety of such a measure. They are not unapprized of the meeting, and can attend if they choose." And, to clinch his argument, he proposed that "Rhode Island might as well be urged to appoint & send deputies."[4] No one rose in defense of an undertaking of that character.

The ill repute of Rhode Island derived mainly from that state's unrestrained experiments with paper money. Rhode Island not only issued paper money freely but also used harsh methods to try to make it circulate. The "legislature passed an act declaring that anyone refusing to take the money at face value would be fined £100 for a first offense and would have to pay a similar fine and lose his rights as a citizen for a second."[5] When the act was challenged, a court declared that it was unconstitutional. Whereupon, the legislature called the judges before it, interrogated them, and dismissed several from office. The legislature was determined to have its paper circulate.

The combination of abundant paper money and Draconian measures to enforce its acceptance brought trade virtually to a halt in Rhode Island. A major American constitutional historian described the situation this way:

The condition of the state during these days was deplorable indeed. The merchants shut their shops and joined the crowd in the bar-rooms; men lounged in the streets or wandered aimlessly about.

A French traveller who passed through Newport about this time gives a dismal picture of the place: idle men standing with folded arms at the corners of the streets; houses falling to ruins; miserable shops offering for sale nothing but a few coarse stuffs ... ; grass growing in the streets; windows stuffed with rags; everything announcing misery, the triumph of paper money, and the influence of bad government. The merchants had closed their stores rather than take payment in paper; farmers from neighboring states did not care to bring their produce.... Some ... sought to starve the tradesmen into a proper appreciation of the simple laws of finance by refusing to bring their produce to market.[6]

But there was more behind the Founders' fears of paper money than contemporary doings in Rhode Island or general pressures for monetary inflation. The country as a whole had only recently suffered the searing aftermath of such an inflation. Much of the War for Independence had been financed with paper money or, more precisely, bills of credit.

A Surge of Continentals

Even before independence had been declared the Continental Congress began to emit bills of credit. These bills carried nothing more than a vague promise that they would at some unspecified time in the future be redeemed, possibly by the states. In effect, they were fiat money, and were never redeemed. As more and more of this Continental currency was issued, 1776-1779, it depreciated in value. This paper was joined by that of the states which were, if anything, freer with their issues than the Congress. In 1777, Congress requested that the states cease to print paper money, but the advice was ignored. They did as Congress did, not what it said.

At first, this surge of paper money brought on what appeared to be a glow of prosperity. As one historian described it, "the country was prosperous....Paper money seemed to be the 'poor man's friend'; to it were ascribed the full employment and the high price of farm products that prevailed during the first years of the war. By 1778, for example, the farmers of New Jersey were generally well off and rapidly getting out of debt, and farms were selling for twice the price they had brought during the period 1765-1775. Trade and commerce were likewise stimulated; despite the curtailment of foreign trade, businessmen had never been so prosperous."[7]

The pleasant glow did not last long, however. It was tarnished first, of course, by the fact that the price of goods people bought began to rise. (People generally enjoy the experience of prices for their goods rising, but they take a contrary view of paying more for what they buy.) Then, as now, some blamed the rise in prices on merchant profiteering.

As the money in circulation increased and expectations of its being redeemed faded, a given amount of money bought less and less. This set the stage for speculative buying, holding on to the goods for a while, and making a large paper profit on them. There were sporadic efforts to control prices as well as widespread efforts to enforce acceptance of the paper money in payment for debts. These efforts, so far as they succeeded, succeeded in causing shortages of goods, creditors to run from debtors trying to pay them in the depreciated currency, and in the onset of suffering.

Runaway Inflation

By 1779, the inflation was nearing the runaway stage. "In August 1778, a Continental paper dollar was valued (in terms of gold and silver) at about twenty-five cents; by the end of 1779, it was worth a penny." "Our dollars pass for less this afternoon than they did this morning," people began to say.[8] George Washington wrote in 1779 that "a wagon load of money will scarcely purchase a wagon load of provisions."[9] It was widely recognized that the cause was the continuing and ever larger emissions of paper money. Congress resolved to issue no more in 1779, but it was all to no avail. Runaway inflation was at hand. In 1781, Congress no longer accepted its own paper money in payment for debts, and the Continentals ceased to have any value at all.

A good portion of the dangers of paper money had been revealed, and reflective people were aware of what had happened. Josiah Quincy wrote George Washington "that there never was a paper pound, a paper dollar, or a paper promise of any kind, that ever yet obtained a general currency but by force or fraud, generally by both."[10] A contemporary historian concluded that the "evils which resulted from the legal tender of the depreciated bills of credit" extended much beyond the immediate assault upon property. "The iniquity of the laws," he said, "estranged the minds of many of the citizens from the habits and love of justice. . . . Truth, honor, and justice were swept away by the overflowing deluge of legal iniquity . . . ."

But the economic consequences of the inflation did not end with the demise of the Continental currency. Instead, it was followed by a deflation, which was the inevitable result of the decrease in the money supply. The deflation was not immediately so drastic as might be supposed. Gold and silver coins generally replaced paper money in 1781. Many of these had been out of circulation, in hiding, so long as they were threatened by tender law requirements to exchange them on a par with the paper money. Once the threat was removed, they circulated. The supply of those in hiding had been augmented over the years by payments for goods by British troops. Large foreign loans, particularly from the French, increased the supply of hard money in the United States in 1781 and 1782. A revived trade with the Spanish, French, and Dutch brought in coins from many lands as well. In addition, Robert Morris's Bank of North America provided paper money redeemable in precious metals in the early years of the decade.

The Impact of Depression

By the middle of the 1780s, however, the deflation was having its impact as a depression. Trade had reopened with Britain, and Americans still showed a distinct preference for British imports. That, plus the fact that the market for American exports in the British West Indies was still closed, resulted in a large imbalance in trade. Americans made up the difference either by borrowing or shipping hard money to Britain. Prices fell to reflect the declining money supply. Those who had gone into debt to buy land at the inflated wartime prices were especially hard hit by the decline in the prices of their produce. Foreclosures were widespread in 1785-1786. This provided the setting for the demands for paper money and other measures to relieve the pressure of the debts. Some people were clamoring for the hair of the dog that had bit them in the first place —

monetary inflation — and several state legislatures had accommodated them.

Though there is evidence that the worst of the depression was over by 1787, if not in the course of 1786,[12] paper money issues and agitations for more were still ongoing when the Constitutional Convention met in Phila-delphia. In any case, those who had absorbed the lessons of recent history were very much concerned to do something to restrain governments from issuing paper money and forcing it into circulation. There were those who met at Philadelphia, too, who took the long view of their task. They hoped to erect a system that would endure, and to do that they wished to guard against the kind of fiscal adventures that produced both unpleasant eco-nomic consequences and political turmoil. Paper money was reckoned to be one of these.

The question of granting power to emit bills of credit came up for discussion twice in the convention. The first time was on August 16, 1787. (The convention had begun its deliberations on May 25, 1787, so it was moving fairly rapidly toward the conclusion when the question arose.) The question was whether or not the United States government should have power to emit bills of credit. Congress had such a power under the Articles of Confederation, and most of the powers held by Congress un-der the Articles were introduced in the convention to be extended to the new government.

Constitutional Convention Debates

Gouverneur Morris of Pennsylvania "moved to strike out 'and emit bills on the credit of the United States'." That is, he proposed to remove the authority for the United States to issue such paper money. "If the United States had credit," Morris said, "such bills would be unnecessary: if they had not, unjust & useless." His motion was seconded by Pierce Butler of South Carolina.

James Madison wondered if it would "not be sufficient to prohibit making them a *tender?* This will remove the temptation to emit them with unjust views. And promissory notes in that shape may in some emergen-cies be best." (Madison's distinction between bills of credit that may be freely circulated and those whose acceptance is forced by tender laws should remind us that paper instruments serving in some fashion as money are not at the heart of the problem. After all, private bills of exchange had

192 / *Clarence B. Carson*

for several centuries been used by tradesmen, and these sometimes changed hands much as money does. They are what we call negotiable instruments, and the variety of these is large. What Madison was getting at more directly, however, was that governments, if they are to borrow money from time to time, may issue notes, and these may be negotiable instruments which may take on some of the character of money in exchanges. But Madison's objection was overcome, as we shall see.)

Gouverneur Morris then observed that "striking out the words will leave room still for notes of a *responsible* minister which will do all the good without the mischief. The Monied interest will oppose the plan of Government, if paper emissions be not prohibited."

However, Morris had moved beyond his motion, which was for removing the power, not specifying a prohibition, and Nathaniel Gorham of Massachusetts brought him back to the point. Gorham said he "was for striking out, without inserting any prohibition. If the words stand they may suggest and lead to the measure."

Not everyone who spoke, however, favored removing the power. George Mason of Virginia "had doubts on the subject. Congress he thought would not have the power unless it were expressed. Though he had a mortal hatred to paper money, yet as he could not foresee all emergences [sic], he was unwilling to tie the hands of the Legislature. He observed that the late war could not have been carried on, had such a prohibition existed."

Nathaniel Gorham tried to reassure Mason and others who might have similar doubts by declaring that "The power so far as it will be necessary or safe, is involved in that of borrowing."

Both Positions Argued

On the other hand, John Francis Mercer of Maryland announced that he "was a friend to paper money, though in the present state & temper in America, he should neither propose nor approve of such a measure. He was consequently opposed to a prohibition of it altogether. It will stamp suspicion on the Government to deny it a discretion on this point. It was impolitic also to excite the opposition of all those who were friends to paper money. The people of property would be sure to be on the side of the plan [the Constitution], and it was impolitic to purchase their further attachment with the loss of the opposite class of Citizens.

Oliver Elsworth of Connecticut pronounced himself of the opposite view. He "thought this a favorable moment to shut and bar the door against paper money. The mischiefs of the various experiments which had been made, were now fresh in the public mind and had excited the disgust of all the respectable part of America. By withholding the power from the new Government more friends of influence would be gained to it than by almost any thing else. Paper money can in no case be necessary. Give the Government credit, and other resources will offer. The power [to emit bills of credit] may do harm, never good."

Edmund Randolph of Virginia still had doubts, for he said that "notwithstanding his antipathy to paper money, [he] could not agree to strike out the words, as he could not foresee all the occasions which might arise.

James Wilson of Pennsylvania favored removing the power: "It will have a most salutary influence on the credit of the United States to remove the possibility of paper money. This expedient can never succeed whilst its mischiefs are remembered, and as long as it can be resorted to, it will be a bar to other resources.

Pierce Butler "remarked that paper was a legal tender in no country in Europe. He was urgent for disarming the Government of such a power.

George Mason, however, "was still averse to tying the hands of the Legislature *altogether.* If there was no example in Europe as just remarked, it might be observed on the other side, that there was none in which the Government was restrained on this head." His fellow delegates forebore to remind Mason that except for Britain there was hardly a government in Europe that was restrained on that or any other head by a written constitution.

In any case, the last remarks were made by men vehemently opposed to the power. George Read of Delaware "thought the words, if not struck out, would be as alarming as the mark of the Beast in Revelations." John Langdon of New Hampshire "had rather reject the whole plan [the Constitution] than retain the three words," by which he meant "and emit bills."

Denying the Power to Emit Bills of Credit

The vote was overwhelmingly in favor of removing the authority of the United States to emit bills of credit. The delegates voted by states, and 9 states voted in favor of the motion while only 2 opposed it. (New York delegates were not in attendance, and Rhode Island, of course, sent none.)

It is a reasonable inference from the discussion that the delegates believed that by voting to strike out the words they had removed the power from the government to emit bills of credit. George Mason, who opposed the motion, admitted as much. Moreover, James Madison explained in a footnote that he voted for it when he "became satisfied that striking out the words would not disable the Government from the use of public notes as far as they could be safe & proper; & would only cut off the pretext for a paper currency, and particularly for making the bills a tender for public or private debts."[13]

The other discussion of paper money took place in connection with the powers to be denied to the states in the Constitution. The committee report had called for the states to be prohibited to emit bills of credit without the consent of the United States Congress. James Wilson and Roger Sherman, who was from Connecticut, "moved to insert after the words 'coin money' the words 'nor emit bills of credit, nor make any thing but gold & silver coin a tender in payment of debts'," thus, as they said, "making these prohibitions absolute, instead of making the measures allowable (as in the XIII article) *with the consent of the Legislature of the U.S.*"

Nathaniel Gorham "thought the purpose would be as well secured by the provision of article XIII which makes the consent of the General Legislature necessary, and that in that mode, no opposition would be excited; whereas an absolute prohibition of paper money would rouse the most desperate opposition from its partizans."

To the contrary, Roger Sherman "thought this a favorable crisis for crushing paper money. If the consent of the Legislature could authorise emissions of it, the friends of paper money, would make every exertion to get into the Legislature in order to licence it."[14]

Eight states voted for the absolution prohibition against states issuing bills of credit. One voted against it, and the other state whose delegation was present was divided. The prohibition, as voted, became a part of the Constitution.

Paper Money Rejected

Three other points may be appropriate. The first has to do with any argument that there might be an implied power for the United States government to issue paper money since it is not specifically prohibited in the

Constitution. Alexander Hamilton, the man credited with advancing the broad construction doctrine, maintained the opposite view in *The Federalist*. While he was making a case against the adding of a bill of rights, his argument was meant to have general validity. He declared that such prohibitions "are not only unnecessary in the proposed Constitution but would even be dangerous. They would contain various exceptions to powers which are not granted; and, on this very account, would afford a colorable pretext to claim more than were granted. For why declare that things shall not be done which there is no power to do."[15] In short, the government does not have all powers not prohibited but only those granted.

Second, this point was driven home by the 10th Amendment when a Bill of Rights was added to the Constitution. It reads, "The powers not delegated to the United States by the Constitution, nor prohibited by it to the States, are reserved to the States respectively, or to the people." The power to emit bills of credit or issue paper money was not delegated to the United States. More, it was specifically not delegated after deliberating upon whether to or not. The power was prohibited to the states. The logical conclusion is that such power as there may be to emit bills of credit was reserved to the people in their private capacities.

And third, not one word has been added to or subtracted from the Constitution since that time affecting the power of government to emit bills of credit or issue paper money.

Since the United States is once again in the toils of an ongoing monetary inflation, it is my hope that this summary review of the experience, words, and deeds of the Founders might shed light on some of the vexing questions surrounding it.

---

1. Actually, the phrase, "fiat money," did not come into use until the 1880s. It might have helped the Founders to specify more precisely what they had in mind to prevent, but they had no such term.

2. E. H. Scott, ed., *Journal of the Federal Convention Kept by James Madison* (Chicago: Albert, Scott and Co., 1893), p. 47.

3. *Ibid.*, p. 60.

4. Charles E. Tansill, ed., *Formation of the Union of the American States* (Washington: Government Printing Office, 1927), p. 306.

5. Merrill Jensen, *The New Nation* (New York: Vintage Books, 1950), p. 324.

6. Andrew C. McLaughlin, *The Confederation and the Constitution* (New York: Collier Books, 1962), pp. 107-08.

7. John C. Miller, *Triumph of Freedom* (Boston: Little, Brown and Co., 1948), p. 438.

8. *Ibid.*, p. 462.

9. Quoted in Albert S. Bolles, *The Financial History of the United States,* vol. 1 (New York: D. Appleton, 1896, 4th ed.), p. 132.

10. *Ibid.*, p. 139.

11. Quoted in *Ibid.,* pp. 177-78.

12. See Jensen, *op. cit.*, pp. 247-48.

13. All the discussion and quotations can be found in Tansill, op. cit., pp. 556-57. While there is no way to know if the record of the debates on this and other matters is complete, nothing has been omitted from Madison's notes.

14. *Ibid.,* pp. 627-38. The committee on style eventually reduced the number of articles in the Constitution to seven, so there is not now an Article XIII, of course.

15. Alexander Hamilton, *et. al.*, *The Federalist Papers* (New Rochelle, N. Y.: Arlington House, n. d.), pp. 513-14.

Index

About *The Freeman*

The Freeman has a long and noble lineage. Albert Jay Nock, the great libertarian journalist, created it in 1920, styling it after *The London Spectator*. It not only covered economic and political issues from a libertarian perspective but also dealt with cultural matters, the theater, concert hall, and the world of literature. During the early twenties, the Nockian *Freeman* was a high water mark of American journalism. It folded in 1924 when the money ran out.

In 1928, *The Freeman* rose renewed as *The New Freeman* under the brilliant editorship of Suzanne LaFollette. It closed its doors in 1931 as one of many victims of the Great Depression. In 1938 it rose again under the editorship of the great Frank Chodorov only to fall prey to World War II. It was reborn after the war with Suzanne LaFollette, Henry Hazlitt, and John Chamberlain as editors.

In January 1956 *The Freeman* found a more lasting home with The Foundation for Economic Education. Under the profound editorship of Paul Poirot it rose to new heights, always espousing the timeless principles of the free society

The *Freeman Classics* series of books reflects these heights, consisting of topical collections of great essays and articles published throughout the years. *Inflation is Theft* is the eleventh volume in the series. Also available: *The Morality of Capitalism, Private Property and Political Control, Prices and Price Controls, Public Education and Indoctrination, Politicized Medicine, Man and Nature, Taxation and Confiscation, Bankers and Regulators, American Unionism*, and *The Spirit of Freedom: Essays in American History*.

—Beth A. Hoffman
Managing Editor

PRICE LIST
Inflation is Theft

Quantity	Price Each
1 copy	$14.95
2-4 copies	12.00
5-49 copies	9.00
50-499 copies	7.50
500 copies	6.00

Please add $3.00 per order for shipping and handling. Send your order, with accompanying check or money order, to the Foundation for Economic Education, 30 South Broadway, Irvington-on-Hudson, New York 10533. Visa and MasterCard telephone and fax orders are welcome; call (914) 591-7230 weekdays or fax (914) 591-8910 anytime.